THE ALCHEMIST

RECIPES AND CONTENT
CURATED BY ARRON TAYLOR,
HANNAH BENTHAM
AND JENNY MCPHEE

ZODIAC AND COCKTAIL PAIRINGS
BY CHARLOTTE SOLOMON
MOONCHILD

EBURY
PRESS

THE ALCHEMIST

COSMIC COCKTAILS

MASTER THE MIXOLOGY OF THE ZODIAC

CONTENTS

'THE FAULT,
DEAR BRUTUS,
IS NOT IN OUR
STARS, BUT
IN OURSELVES,
THAT WE ARE
UNDERLINGS'

JULIUS CAESAR,
ACT ONE, SCENE TWO

We started writing our first cocktail book compendium at the end of 2019, as a celebration of ten years of molecular mixology at The Alchemist. The book was a joyful journey back through some of our guests' favourite concoctions as well as a retrospective of the brilliant bartenders and the wild and wonderful techniques that they employ, to bring our brand of alchemic theatre to venues across the land.

… And then it was 2020 and all of a sudden, our world stopped spinning.

The Alchemist thought long and hard in that period about our place in Space and in Time; we missed the magic of drinks delivery IRL, of preparation and process behind the bar, the energy and optimism pre-shifts, the camaraderie of all-action Saturdays and the human pleasure of tenderly tending the bar on Tuesdays. Mostly, we missed the reactions, the awe and the wonder, and sometimes the simple delight that a well-crafted cocktail could bring to a guest.

And yet we knew that the cosmos moves in mysterious ways, so we chose not to suffer the slings and arrows of outrageous fortune, as the bard (sort of) said. Instead, we spent time dreaming impossible cocktail dreams and set to work to create bolder, brighter, more brilliant drinks than ever before. Cocktails to take you … out of this world.

Today, five years on, we've made concoctions that levitate before your very eyes, creations that kiss you back (!) and liquid oysters that put the 'shoot the moon' in shooters.

We've also thought much more about our place in this world as it continues to rapidly evolve around us; endeavouring to tread more carefully and lightly as we go about our craft. We've closed the loop on many of our cocktails, upcycling wasted citrus into marmalades and excess greens into simple shrubs. Waste wine is transformed into syrups that add depth to our serves. Passionfruits have gone, and with them the many thousands of air miles, but the passion has not. We're going to demonstrate this later on in this book.

So, volume two of The Alchemist is here to help you enter a new dimension as you learn to shake, spin, smoke and serve a brand-new collection of our most cosmic creations. And because we're all star-crossed lovers at heart (sorry again, Shakespeare), we've categorised each drink through the zodiac so you can be sure of party-perfect planetary alignment.

EQUIPMENT

BAR BLADE

A bar blade is no ordinary bottle opener: it is a speed opener, allowing you to open ten bottles of beer in 4.2 seconds (with practice!). We use it as a mark of seniority: as a bartender works through our progression scheme, they earn a personalised Alchemist bar blade, each with its own unique number.

BOSTON TIN & GLASS COCKTAIL SHAKER

We choose to create our cocktails using a Boston tin and glass shaker, rather than a tin-on-tin shaker, as we like to add a dash of theatre to everything we do. It means that, whether your cocktail is shaken or stirred, you're always able to witness a glimpse of the production.

When it comes to 'the art of the shake', build your ingredients into the glass, then slide on the tin at a slight angle and twist slightly while pushing down to seal. Hold the bottom of the glass securely with one hand while holding the top of the tin with the other. Sling the tin in one rapid motion over your shoulder and back down to lock (a bonus is that this makes you look pretty cool). Turn the shaker upside down so the glass is facing upwards, then shake.

To unlock the tin, make sure the glass is facing upwards and use the palm of your hand to gently smack the tin where it meets the glass.

HAWTHORNE STRAINER & FINE STRAINER

Two of the most essential pieces of equipment for any bartender. Place your Hawthorne strainer in the top of your Boston tin, with the coil facing downwards, and use it to hold back the ice as you strain your shaken cocktail into your glass. If your shaken cocktails are being served straight up (without ice), use in combination with a fine strainer to remove any ice shards or pulp.

BAR SPOON

The bar spoon is the crème de la crème of spoons. The long, spiralled handle makes light work of mixing drinks, even in the tallest glassware, and the flat end works perfectly for layering spirits in cocktails to help you show off some artistic flair. What's more, a bar spoon holds about 5ml of liquid (the same as a teaspoon), so it can be used to measure out those smaller amounts of liquid that can be difficult to accurately do in a shot glass.

MUDDLER

We use a muddler for mashing, grinding or crushing ingredients such as fruit, herbs or spices. Essentially, this breaks them down, releasing their juices, oils and flavour compounds.

JULEP STRAINER

After stirring drinks in the glass part of your Boston shaker, use a julep strainer as you transfer the drink into your glass. Place the strainer, curved side up, over the ice (the glass should be almost full to the brim with ice) and hold it down with your index finger as you pour.

BLENDER

A good-quality blender is an important piece of equipment in any bartender's arsenal. Whether you are prepping batches or foams, or simply blending up a strawberry daiquiri on a hot summer's day, it's important to make sure you have a high-powered blender to help get the job done.

We use blenders in different ways to get different results. Blending with a scoop of crushed ice will create a frozen cocktail, while blending with three ice cubes will help to dilute the cocktail slightly, at the same time creating a fluffy texture and velvety mouthfeel.

FLAVOUR BLASTER

We use this innovative piece of kit to create our vapour bubbles on iconic serves such as Pop Notch (page 118) and Cherry Poppins (page 54). Now available in a mini size for at-home use.

JIGGER

A double-ended tool used for measuring and pouring liquid. The large end holds 50ml while the smaller end holds 25ml.

MEASURING JUG

A glass measuring jug is helpful when batching up serves for large-scale events.

ULTRA-PRECISION SCALES

One of the most important pieces of equipment that we use on a daily basis is a set of good-quality, ultra-precision scales, accurate to the nearest 0.01g. Many of the powders we use are extremely powerful in small quantities and a variation of just 0.1g can change a drink drastically, so it's important to be accurate. You can pick up a set of these scales fairly easily online and they are generally inexpensive, so are definitely worth the investment.

LIGHTER

An essential for an Alchemist bartender, used for lighting woodchips, spritzing oils from citrus peel and lighting flash paper.

ICE BALL MOULDS

There are lots of shapes available, we love a classic large ice ball.

SYRINGE

We use a syringe to extract liquids and dispense in certain drinks like Pear-ple Rain (page 64). A pipette would also work well.

OAK BARREL

We use barrels to age various cocktails, such as Negronis and Pineapple Daquiris. They can be sourced from Master of Malt or Urban Bar. The more you use the better flavours will flourish.

DEHYDRATOR

This is a great piece of kit that pulls moisture from fruit/veg at a low temperature, preserving nutrients and ensuring no mould or bacteria grow. We use this machine to create dehydrated citrus peel from chopping-board waste.

If you don't have a dehydrater you can achieve a similar end product by using an oven. Set to the lowest temperature and place cut citrus or fruit in for 6–8 hours.

Air fryers also offer this function, please check instructions for temperature and times.

FLASH PAPER & STRING

As fun and cool as this is, you must take care while handling as misuse could cause burns. This is extremely flammable and should be used in small amounts.

It's good practice to store them in metal containers and cut using scissors when needed. You could also store this in a cool, dry place.

DRY ICE

Unlike other chemicals, dry ice has no liquid stage, going straight from a solid to a gas. This means it interacts with our delicious liquids in interesting ways. The process by which dry ice changes to a gas is known as sublimation. The gas it makes comes in the form of a mysterious white fog, but there are a number of magical reasons we use it in addition to its visual impact.

- AROMA
  When you introduce dry ice to a warm liquid infused with fresh fruit the gas carries the aroma and envelops the room. Visually, it impresses, but it's also a multisensory experience that gets you salivating as your drink is made.

- CARBONATION
  Fizzy drinks are carbonated with CO_2. The addition of dry ice to a drink lightly carbonates it, changing the mouthfeel, and alters the flavour, adding the acidity you encounter in sparkling drinks.

- TEMPERATURE
  A warm liquid reacts more quickly with dry ice, producing more aroma and fog. Dry ice is also a way of chilling the liquid without diluting it or changing the flavour in the way normal ice does.

- SAFETY
  You must not drink the dry ice; allow it to dissolve and dissipate first. Do not breathe dry ice mist in directly and always handle the pellets with gloves. Do not store dry ice in a sealed container, or a freezer, but in the container provided by the manufacturer.

BLOWTORCH

A useful piece of equipment, whether you use it to torch a cinnamon stick for a sweet and spicy aroma, to caramelise a lime or to toast a Meringue Foam garnish. There's something about adding fire to any situation that always gives that 'wow' factor and is a guaranteed crowd-pleaser.

FOAMER

We create our foams using an iSi foamer and N^2O gas, which allows us to create velvety and stiff-peaked foams.

SMOKE GUN

A smoke gun is an amazing piece of equipment that allows us to create thick, flavourful smoke, which is perfect for infusing cocktails while creating a sense of theatre. We use oak woodchips, which give a classic smokey flavour and aroma, but you can experiment with other types of woodchips in order to get different results.

Pour the woodchips into the hole in the top of the smoke gun and turn it on to full. Direct the nozzle into the glass you want to smoke and use a lighter or match to light the woodchips. Smoke will start to billow from the nozzle. Turn off the smoker once you have achieved the desired amount of smoke, then discard the woodchips.

CREATING SMOKE WITHOUT A GUN

- LIGHT SMOKE

  Place some woodchips on a heat-resistant surface, such as a baking tray. Light them using a lighter flame or blowtorch until they are gently smouldering. Place your glass over the smouldering chips and leave to infuse for a few minutes. This process will lightly coat the glass with smoke and create a wonderful smokey flavour.

- HEAVY SMOKE

  Place the woodchips on a heat-resistant surface, such as a baking tray. Light them using a lighter flame or blowtorch until gently smouldering. Take a carafe or a stirring jar and place it over the top of the chips. Allow to infuse for a few minutes, then continue to mix the cocktail in the carafe or jar.

BATCHES, MIXES & SPHERIFICATION

Store-cupboard essentials for the modern alchemist. Here you will find a list of our most necessary mixes and dilutions and once prepped they can be used in many of our cocktails throughout the book

CITRIC ACID DILUTION

This dilution works well for adding a citrus element to a drink without the cloudiness you get from lemon or lime juice.

MAKES 750ML
— 20G CITRIC ACID POWDER
— 750ML FILTERED WATER

Place the ingredients in a blender and blend for 30 seconds, or until the powder is completely dissolved. Pour into a sterilised bottle. It will keep for at least a month in the fridge, which makes it a great alternative to fresh citrus as you don't need to use it right away.

LEMON MIX

This technique consists of muddling sugar into citrus peels and leaving it for a few hours or overnight, allowing the sugar to extract the oils from the peels and creating a delicious syrup.

MAKES 750ML
— 20G FINELY GRATED LEMON ZEST OR PEEL
— 500ML LEMON JUICE
— 200G CASTER SUGAR
— 5ML (1 TEASPOON) BITTER TRUTH LEMON BITTERS

Add the lemon zest or peel to a large jug. Add the juice to the zest and leave to infuse for 30 minutes or overnight. After infusing, add the caster sugar and bitters and stir to dissolve. Once all of the sugar has dissolved, strain through a fine strainer to remove any zest, then pour the liquid into a sterilised bottle. It will keep for 4 days in the fridge.

ACIDIFIED CRANBERRY JUICE

Adding citrus acid delivers a tartness to the cranberry juice

MAKES 200ML
— 8G CITRIC ACID POWDER
— 200ML CRANBERRY JUICE

Add both ingredients into a blender and blend for 30 seconds. Pour into a sterilised bottle. This will keep for 2 days in the fridge.

MAGIC MIX

A clever mix that is the magic behind our most-loved serve

MAKES 700ML
- 1LITRE FILTERED WATER
- 1 RED CABBAGE
- 20G BICARBONATE OF SODA

Add the water to a large saucepan and bring to the boil. Chop the cabbage into chunks and add to a litre of boiling water then add the bicarbonate of soda. Let this boil for 2 hours, remove from the heat and leave to cool at room temperature for 1 hour. Then strain out the cabbage pieces using a sieve. This will last for 1 day and should be kept cool in the fridge.

TONY'S CHOCOLATE MILK

Our housemade chocolate oat milk. We use Tony's Chocolonely because the chocolate is delicious and we love their ethos.

MAKES 750ML
- 180G MILK CHOCOLATE (WE USE TONY'S CHOCOLONELY)
- 750ML OAT MILK
- YOU WILL ALSO NEED A SUGAR THERMOMETER

Place a heatproof bowl over a small pan filled with water, making sure the water does not touch the bottom of the bowl. Over a medium heat, bring the water to the boil. Break your chocolate into small chunks and add to the bowl. Stir regularly until melted.

Separately, heat the oat milk in a pan to 65°C (using a thermometer), then pour into the bowl of melted chocolate over the heat and stir until it is well mixed. Turn off the heat and allow to cool.

Once cooled, strain into a clean bottle. This will keep for 1 week in the fridge.

PORNSTAR BATCH

We add vermouth to mature and enhance the overall flavour of our Pornstar Martini. This is good to have on hand when entertaining.

MAKES 750ML
- 250ML PASSOÃ
- 250ML WHITE VERMOUTH
- 250ML CITRIC ACID DILUTION (PAGE 14)

Add all the ingredients to a jug and stir well to mix. Strain into a clean bottle. This will keep for 1 week in the fridge.

MULLED BELLINI BATCH

We use waste red wine to create this syrup. Add 25ml of this to a glass of fizz for that festive feel.

MAKES 700ML
- 350ML RED WINE REDUCTION (PAGE 31)
- 350ML MONIN SPICED RED BERRIES SYRUP
- 1 TEASPOON GOLD METALLIC POWDER

Add all the ingredients to a jug and stir well to combine. Strain into a clean bottle. This will keep for 1 week in the fridge.

ALCHEMIST MARMALADE

We use waste citrus which is combined with sugar to create a sustainable delicious marmalade.

MAKES 1L
- 1KG CITRUS FRUIT
- 800ML FILTERED WATER
- 1KG CASTER SUGAR

Chop the fruit into roughly 1cm pieces. Transfer to a medium pan and add 400ml of the filtered water. Bring to the boil and cook for 30 minutes, or until the fruit is soft. Turn off the hob and take the pan to the sink, then pour all of the contents through a strainer to catch all the solid pieces, discarding the liquid.

Return the cooked fruit to the pan with the remaining 400ml of the water and add the caster sugar. Bring to the boil once again and leave to simmer for a further 30 minutes to ensure the sugar dissolves. After 30 minutes, turn off the hob and allow the marmalade to cool.

Once cooled, transfer the marmalade to an airtight jar. This will keep for 2 weeks in the fridge.

PINEAPPLE CAVIAR

Our caviars create an eye-catching addition to any drink. Make this ahead of time and refrigerate until you are ready to make cocktails.

MAKES 150ML
- 100ML ALGINATE MIX (RIGHT)
- 50ML SIMPLE SUGAR SYRUP (PAGE 28)
- 1ML PINEAPPLE FLAVOUR DROPS
- 0.1G RED COLOURING POWDER

Combine all the ingredients in a bowl and stir well to mix. Transfer to a clean bottle. This caviar will keep for at least 4 days in the fridge.

CALCIUM SOLUTION

This dilution can be used as a calcium bath during the spherification process.

MAKES 750ML
- 22.5G CALCIUM LACTATE POWDER
- 750ML FILTERED WATER

Place the ingredients in a blender and blend for 30 seconds, or until the powder is completely dissolved. Pour into a sterilised bottle. It will keep for 3 days in the fridge.

ALGINATE MIX

Sodium alginate is a product extracted from algae which, when combined with water, forms a gel-like substance which can be used to create our caviar and jelly spheres.

MAKES 750ML
- 9G SODIUM ALGINATE POWDER
- 750ML FILTERED WATER

Place the ingredients in a blender and blend for 30 seconds, or until smooth. Pour into a sterilised bottle. This will keep in the fridge for up to 4 days.

STRAWBERRY JELLY

This jelly is used in The Trifle (page 52) and is a playful take on a jello shot. We use a gelatine alternative which makes these jellies vegetarian.

MAKES 8
- 100ML STRAWBERRY SYRUP
- 100ML FILTERED WATER
- 2G ULTRAGEL
- YOU WILL ALSO NEED 8 SERVING GLASSES

Place the strawberry syrup, water and UltraGel in a saucepan over a medium heat. Stir well to combine and warm through for about 5 minutes, or until visibly warm but not boiling.

Once cool, pour the mixture into 8 serving glasses and place them in the fridge for at least 3 hours, or until set. This will keep for a week in the fridge.

GARNISHES

The final flourish to any great drink is a well-considered garnish. From edible glass to dehydrated fruits and flowers, the possibilities are endless.

IRON BRU LOLLIPOPS

A fun garnish using an iconic Scottish delicacy.

MAKES 10
- 200G ISOMALT
- 10ML (2 TEASPOONS) IRN BRU REDUCTION (PAGE 31)
- 4ML IRN BRU FLAVOUR DROPS
- YOU WILL ALSO NEED 10 HEATPROOF LOLLIPOP SILICONE MOULDS

Place the isomalt in a small saucepan over a medium heat and stir until it melts. Add the syrup and flavour drops and stir.

Once melted, turn off the heat and allow the mixture to cool for 30 seconds, then pour into the moulds. Careful, this will be very hot. Add the lollipop sticks to the moulds while keeping your hands safely away from the mixture. Leave to cool for 30 minutes.

Transfer to the fridge for 3 hours, or until set. Once set, carefully remove the lollipops from the moulds and store in an airtight container, separated by sheets of baking paper. They will keep for 3 days in the fridge. Enjoy!

LIME SHERBET AIR

Our take on a floaty lime cloud.

MAKES 100ML
- 50ML LIME SHERBET SYRUP
- 50ML FILTERED WATER
- 4 DROPS OF ULTRAFOAM

Add all the ingredients to a glass and mix thoroughly with a spoon.

DISCO LOLLIES

An orange-flavoured lolly, watch out for a colour-changing tongue.

MAKES 10
- 200G ISOMALT
- 10ML (2 TEASPOONS) BRISTOL SYRUP COMPANY DISCO BLUE
- 2ML ORANGE FLAVOUR DROPS
- YOU WILL ALSO NEED 10 HEATPROOF LOLLIPOP SILICONE MOULDS

Place the isomalt in a small saucepan over a medium heat and stir until it melts. Add the Disco Blue and orange drops and stir.

Once melted, follow the instructions for cooling and adding the mixture to the moulds as in the IRN BRU Lollipops recipe (left).

INDIGO DROPS
Flavourless, colourful drops that create a black rain-like effect.

MAKES 250ML
- 5G BLACK COLOURING POWDER
- 1G SILVER METALLIC POWDER
- 250ML FILTERED WATER

Add all the ingredients to a jug and stir well to mix.

BATTENBERG AIR
A dreamy airy topping that tastes like that classic cake.

MAKES 150ML
- 50ML AMARETTO
- 50ML ALMOND SYRUP
- 50ML WATER
- 6 DROPS OF ULTRAFOAM

Add all the ingredients to a glass and mix thoroughly with a spoon.

BASIL GLASS
Our playful version of edible glass, which is used to garnish the Basil Smash (page 83).

MAKES 3
- 90G ISOMALT
- 0.1G GOLD METALLIC POWDER
- 3 FRESH BASIL LEAVES
- YOU WILL ASO NEED 3 × 15CM ROUND SILICONE MOULDS

Place the isomalt in a small saucepan over a medium heat and stir until it melts.

Once melted, turn off the heat and allow the mixture to cool slightly for 30 seconds, then pour into the silicone moulds. Careful, this will be very hot. Leave to cool for 30 minutes.

Transfer to the fridge for 3 hours to cool and set. Once set, carefully remove the basil glass and transfer to an airtight container, separated by sheets of baking paper. Store in the fridge until needed.

When ready to serve, lightly press a fresh basil leaf to the side of the serving glass, ensuring it sticks, then top the drink with the disc. They will last for 3 days in the fridge.

VIMTO JELLY
A cheeky garnish for a cheeky drink.

MAKES 6
- 100ML VIMTO
- 50ML FILTERED WATER
- 5G CASTER SUGAR
- 2G ULTRAGEL
- YOU WILL ALSO NEED 6 SHOT GLASSES

Place the Vimto and water in a saucepan over a medium heat. Stir well to combine and warm through for about 5 minutes, or until visibly warm but not boiling.

In a small bowl, mix together the caster sugar and UltraGel until combined.

When the liquid in the saucepan is hot, slowly add the gel and sugar mixture, a little at a time, stirring continuously. Once it's all dissolved, turn off the heat and allow the mix to cool.

Once cooled, pour the mixture into the shot glasses and place them in the fridge for at least 3 hours, or until set.

EGG GLASS

A creative garnish for our take on a Manhattan.

MAKES 5–8
— 385G ISOMALT
— 0.2G YELLOW COLOURING POWDER
— 0.7G WHITE COLOURING POWDER
— YOU WILL ALSO NEED 5–8 HEATPROOF
  PETIT FOUR MOULDS
— YOU WILL ALSO NEED 5–8 15CM ROUND
  SILICONE MOULDS

For the 'egg yolks', place 160g of the isomalt into a small saucepan over a medium heat with the yellow colouring powder, then stir until it melts. Once melted, turn off the heat and allow the mixture to cool slightly for 30 seconds, then pour into the petit four moulds. Careful, this will be very hot. Leave to cool for 30 minutes. Transfer to the fridge for 3 hours to cool and set.

Once set, you can start the 'egg whites'. Place the remaining 225g of isomalt into a small saucepan over a medium heat with the white colouring powder, then stir until it melts. Once melted, turn off the heat and allow the mixture to cool slightly for 30 seconds, then pour into the round moulds. Careful, this will be very hot. Gently move the moulds so the mixture touches 3 sides to look like an egg.

Remove the set yolks from the moulds and carefully place these on top of your egg discs. Leave to cool for 30 minutes. Transfer to the fridge for 3 hours to cool and set.

Carefully remove the egg glass. Store in an airtight container, separated by sheets of baking paper.

ELECTRIC SYRUP

A unique syrup that creates an electrifying sensation.

MAKES 200ML
— 200ML GIN
— 30 SECHUAN BUTTONS®
— 0.5G RED COLOURING POWDER

Add all the ingredients to a jug and stir well to mix. Leave for 24 hours for the buttons to infuse. Pass the liquid through a fine strainer into a clean bottle, discarding the buttons. This will keep in a fridge for 7 days.

GOLD CHOCOLATE BANANAS

An edible chocolate garnish for a decadent drink.

MAKES 6
— 180G MILK CHOCOLATE
— EDIBLE GOLD POWDER
— YOU WILL ALSO NEED BANANA-SHAPED
  SILICONE MOULDS

Lightly coat the mould with the gold powder. Melt the chocolate over a bain marie, stirring regularly. Once fully melted, pour into your moulds and place in the fridge for 2 hours to set.

TOFFEE APPLES

A baby apple covered in sweet sugar glass.

MAKES 15
— 150G ISOMALT
— 0.4G RED COLOURING POWDER
— 15 BABY APPLES
— YOU WILL ALSO NEED 15 HEATPROOF PETIT
  FOUR MOULDS

Place the isomalt and red colouring powder in a saucepan over a medium heat and stir until it melts. Once melted, turn off the heat and allow the mixture to cool slightly for 30 seconds, then pour into the petit four moulds. Careful, this will be very hot.

Ensuring your fingers are at a safe distance, hold the stem of each baby apple and dip it into the red isomalt mixture until fully submerged, then leave to set for 3 hours on a silicone sheet.

Once set, store in an airtight container, separated by baking paper. These will last 3 days in the fridge.

DEHYDRATED CITRUS WEDGES
We like to use discarded chopping-board fruit which would otherwise go to waste to make dehydrated fruit garnishes as well as infusions.

– VARIOUS WASTE CITRUS FRUIT OF YOUR CHOICE

Chop the fruit into wedges or slices around 1cm thick. Lay out the slices on a baking sheet lined with baking paper and place in a dehydrator or an oven set to 55°C/Gas mark ⅛ for 12 hours to dehydrate.

When fully dehydrated, transfer to an airtight jar and seal, to ensure they keep dry. Store at room temperature.

BLACKCURRANT BALLS
A process known as reverse spherification, these squidgy balls are incredibly fun to pop.

MAKES 6
– 9G CALCIUM LACTATE POWDER
– 60ML BOILING WATER
– 150ML CRANBERRY JUICE
– 90ML CASSIS SYRUP
– 0.6G BLACKCURRANT FLAVOUR DROPS
– 600ML ALGINATE MIX (PAGE 17)

– YOU WILL ALSO NEED 6 ROCK GLASSES, 6 HEATPROOF PETIT FOUR MOULDS AND A THERMOMETER

In a jug, mix together the calcium lactate powder and boiling water until the powder has dissolved. Careful, this will be hot. Add the cranberry juice, cassis syrup and blackcurrant drops and stir to combine. Divide the mixture between the petit four moulds. Transfer to the freezer and freeze for 4 hours or until completely frozen.

Once frozen, heat the alginate mix in a saucepan until it reaches 70°C on a thermometer. Pour 100ml of the mixture into each rocks glass.

Drop one frozen ball into each glass of alginate and allow it to sink to the bottom. After about a minute, a jelly skin should begin to form around the ball. Wait for 3 minutes, then carefully strain out the balls. Put the balls straight into a bowl of warm water to wash off any excess alginate.

Store the balls for up to a week in a sterilised, airtight jar with 250ml water in the fridge until ready to serve.

BATH BOMBS
Our take on a fizzy bath bomb which you can actually drink.

MAKES 24
– 56G BICARBONATE OF SODA
– 66G CITRIC ACID POWDER
– 50G ASCORBIC ACID
– 0.1G BLUE COLOURING POWDER
– 0.5G GOLD COLOURING POWDER
– 0.7G RED COLOURING POWDER
– 16G ARTIFICIAL SWEETENER
– 5ML (1 TEASPOON) STRAWBERRY FLAVOUR DROPS
– YOU WILL ALSO NEED 24 SMALL SEMI-CIRCLE MOULDS

Wearing gloves, mix all the ingredients together until the mixture feels like wet sand. Leave aside for 20 minutes.

Turn on your dehydrator to 65°C. Spoon the mixture into your semi-circle moulds, leaving a 2mm clearance at the top. Place into the dehydrator for 15 minutes.

Remove the moulds and recompress with 2 fingers. Leave to air-dry for a further 20 minutes, then remove from moulds and store in an airtight container.

WHITE CHOCOLATE ICE LOLLIES
Mini white chocolate ice cream garnishes.

MAKES 4
- 100ML WHITE CHOCOLATE FOAM (PAGE 32)
- 25ML AMARETTO
- 0.5G XANTHAN GUM
- YOU WILL ALSO NEED 4 ICE LOLLY MOULDS AND LOLLIPOP STICKS

Mix all the ingredients and portion into the ice lolly moulds, then add the lollipop sticks. Freeze for 4 hours.

LAVENDER AIR
A light floaty topping with a fragrant lavender scent.

MAKES 150ML
- 100ML LAVENDER SYRUP
- 50ML FILTERED WATER
- 6 DROPS OF ULTRAFOAM

Add all the ingredients to a glass and mix thoroughly with a spoon.

ROOIBOS JELLY
A fun jelly infused with tea.

MAKES 20
- 15G ROOIBOS LOOSE LEAF TEA
- 500ML BOILING WATER
- 50ML STRAWBERRY SYRUP
- 55G CASTER SUGAR
- 4G ULTRAGEL
- YOU WILL ALSO NEED 20 SHOT GLASSES

Place the tea in a heatproof jug and pour over the boiling water, then infuse for 30 minutes. Pass the tea through a fine strainer into a saucepan, keeping the liquid but discarding the tea leaves.

Set the saucepan over a medium heat, add the strawberry syrup to the tea, stir well to combine and warm through for about 5 minutes, or until visibly warm but not boiling.

In a small bowl, mix together the caster sugar and UltraGel until combined. When the liquid in the saucepan is hot, slowly add the gel and sugar mixture, a little at a time, stirring continuously. Once it's all dissolved, turn off the heat and allow to cool.

Once cool, pour the mixture into shot glasses and set them in the fridge for at least 3 hours.

DEHYDRATED STRAWBERRIES
Why not, to use discarded chopping-board fruit?

- CHOPPING-BOARD WASTE OR A PUNNET OF STRAWBERRIES

Chop the fruit into wedges or slices around 1cm thick. Lay out the slices on a baking sheet lined with baking paper and place in a dehydrator or oven at 55°C/Gas mark ⅛ for 12 hours to dehydrate.

When fully dehydrated, transfer to an airtight jar and seal, to ensure they keep dry. Store at room temperature.

INFUSIONS

An infusion is a creative way to elevate your favourite spirits with fresh and vibrant flavours. Whether you are looking add depth to a cocktail or explore new, exciting taste combinations, this collection of infused spirit recipes offers something for every palate.

PEANUT BUTTER RUM

MAKES 700ML

- 700ML RUM
- 60G SMOOTH PEANUT BUTTER

Add the rum and peanut butter to a blender and blend until mixed. Filter through coffee filter paper into a clean bottle. This will keep for a month at room temperature. Shake before use.

STRAWBERRY LACES GIN

MAKES 700ML

- 112G STRAWBERRY LACES
- 700ML GIN

Add the strawberry laces to the gin bottle and leave to infuse for 24 hours.

Strain through a fine strainer into a clean bottle, discarding the laces. This will keep for a month at room temperature. Shake before use.

MANGO CHILLI TEQUILA

MAKES 700ML

- ½ MANGO , PEELED AND CHOPPED
- 2 CHILLIES, CHOPPED
- 700ML TEQUILA

Chop the mango into slices around 1cm thick. Lay out on a baking sheet lined with baking paper and place in a dehydrator or oven at 55°C/Gas mark ⅛ for 12 hours to dehydrate.

When ready, add your dehydrated mango and chopped chillies to the tequila and leave to infuse for 24 hours.

Strain through a fine strainer into a clean bottle, discarding the mango and chillies. This will keep for a month at room temperature. Shake before use.

SWEET GARLIC VODKA

MAKES 700ML

- 2 GARLIC CLOVES
- 2 TEASPOONS DEMERARA SUGAR
- 700ML VODKA

Chop the garlic into slices and add to a small saucepan over a medium heat. Add the sugar and cook until caramelised. Once caramelised, add to the vodka and leave to infuse for 24 hours.

Strain through a fine strainer into a clean bottle, discarding the garlic.

MINCE PIE RUM
MAKES 700ML
- 410G MINCEMEAT
- 700ML RUM

Add the mincemeat to a bowl and pour the rum over. Stir to combine and leave to infuse for 24 hours.

Strain into a jug through a fine strainer to remove the mincemeat, then filter through coffee filter paper into a sterilised bottle. This will keep for a month at room temperature. Shake before use.

LIME LEAF-INFUSED VODKA OR GIN
MAKES 700ML
- 30G MAKRUT LIME LEAVES
- 700ML VODKA OR GIN

Add the lime leaves to the spirit bottle and leave to infuse for 24 hours.

Strain through a fine strainer into a clean bottle. This will keep for a month at room temperature. Shake before use.

CINNAMON TEQUILA
MAKES 500ML
- 500ML TEQUILA
- 45G CINNAMON STICKS
- YOU WILL ALSO NEED A FOAMER AND 2 × N_2O WHIPPERS (OPTIONAL)

WITH A FOAMER
Add all the ingredients to a foamer. Charge with a N_2O whipper and leave for 1 hour.

Carefully release all the gas from the foamer by lightly holding the trigger with the nozzle facing upwards. Once all gas has been released, remove the lid and strain through a fine strainer into a clean bottle.

WITHOUT A FOAMER
Add all the ingredients to a jug and leave to infuse for 24 hours.

Strain through a fine strainer into a clean bottle.

LEMONGRASS GIN
MAKES 700ML
- 700ML GIN
- 50G LEMONGRASS STALKS

Pour the gin into a blender. Cutting off the tops of the lemongrass stalks, add to the blender and blend for 30 seconds. Filter the liquid through coffee filter paper into a clean bottle.

This will keep for a month at room temperature where the flavours will continue to infuse.

SYRUPS & REDUCTIONS

Syrups are the base for most of your favourite cocktails, adding sweetness and viscosity. A Simple Sugar Syrup is your starting base, then swap in different ingredients to provide depth or sharpness.

SIMPLE SUGAR SYRUP

The most prevalent syrup in your back bar, you will find this in most classic cocktail recipes.

MAKES 700ML
- 500ML CASTER SUGAR
- 500ML BOILING WATER

Place the sugar and water in a small saucepan over a medium heat. Stir continuously until all the sugar is dissolved, then transfer to a clean heatproof bottle.

Leave to cool before using. This syrup will keep for at least a month in the fridge.

HONEY SYRUP

MAKES 250ML
- 125ML HONEY
- 125ML WARM WATER

Add the ingredients to a blender and blend for 30 seconds.

Strain through a fine strainer into a clean bottle. This will keep for a week in the fridge.

COLD BREW COFFEE

MAKES 700ML
- 30G FRESH GROUND COFFEE
- 56G CASTER SUGAR
- 700ML BOILING WATER

Add the coffee grounds to a heatproof jug, sprinkle over the sugar and leave for 4 hours to allow the sugar to pull the oil from the coffee. Pour in the boiling water and mix well, then leave to cool for 1 hour.

Filter through coffee filter paper into a clean bottle. This will keep for a week in the fridge.

FIRE SYRUP

A ruby red, metallic syrup.

MAKES 750ML
- 275ML PASSIONFRUIT SYRUP
- 275ML RASPBERRY SYRUP
- 1 TEASPOON RUBY METALLIC POWDER
- 1½ TEASPOONS ULTRATEX POWDER
- 200ML BOILING WATER

Place the passionfruit and raspberry syrups and ruby metallic powder in a blender and blend to combine.

In a jug, mix together the Ultratex powder and boiling water and stir until smooth. Pour this mixture into the syrup mixture and stir well to combine. Transfer to a clean bottle. This will keep for at least a month in the fridge.

CUCUMBER & MINT SYRUP
MAKES 750ML
- 133G CUCUMBER
- 67G WHOLE MINT SPRINGS
- 500G AGAVE SYRUP
- 250ML BOILING WATER

Dice the cucumber into small squares, then add the cucumber and mint sprigs to a heatproof jug or container. Add the agave syrup and boiling water and stir to combine. Leave to infuse for 1–2 hours.

Strain through a fine strainer into a clean bottle. This will keep for 1 week in the fridge.

MALT SYRUP
MAKES 700ML
- 350ML MALT EXTRACT
- 350ML WARM WATER

Place the malt extract and warm water in a blender and blend to combine. Transfer to a clean bottle and allow to settle before using. Store in the fridge until read to use. This will keep for at least a month.

SALINE SOLUTION
Adds salt to a serve for a consistent finish.

MAKES 125ML
- 25G SEA SALT
- 125ML WATER

Add both ingredients to a blender and blend for 30 seconds.

Strain through a fine strainer into a clean bottle. This will keep in the fridge for 1 week.

PLUM & HONEY SYRUP
MAKES 250ML
- 4 PLUMS
- 2 TEASPOONS DEMERARA SUGAR
- 130G CASTER SUGAR
- 250ML BOILING WATER
- 1 TEASPOON HONEY

Cut the plums into small chunks and place in a small saucepan over a low heat. Sprinkle over the demerara sugar and cook until caramelised.

Add the caster sugar, water and honey and bring to the boil, then turn off the heat and allow to infuse and cool for 30 minutes.

Strain through a fine strainer into a clean bottle. This will keep for 4 days in the fridge.

CARDAMOM SYRUP
MAKES 500ML
- 500ML SIMPLE SUGAR SYRUP (PAGE 28)
- 20G CARDAMOM SEEDS

Add all the ingredients to a saucepan over a low heat and cook gently to infuse for 30 minutes.

Strain through a fine strainer into a heatproof tub and leave to cool for 1 hour. Once cooled, pour into a clean bottle. This will keep for 1 week in the fridge.

PEPPERCORN SYRUP

MAKES 500ML
- 75G BLACK PEPPERCORNS
- 250ML CASTER SUGAR
- 250ML BOILING WATER

Add all the ingredients to a blender and blend for 30 seconds, then leave to infuse for 30 minutes.

Filter through coffee filter paper into a clean bottle and transfer to the fridge. This syrup will keep for at least 1 month in the fridge.

RED WINE REDUCTION

MAKES 700ML
- 500ML RED WINE
- 4G DRIED ROSEMARY
- 4 DRIED BAY LEAVES
- 4G DRIED THYME
- 125G CASTER SUGAR
- 100ML DARK RUM

Add all the ingredients to a saucepan set over a low heat and cook gently, with the lid on, to infuse for 30 minutes.

Strain through a fine strainer into a heatproof tub and leave to cool for 1 hour. Once cooled, pour into a clean bottle. This will keep in the fridge for 7 days.

GUINNESS REDUCTION

MAKES 500ML
- 1 × 440ML GUINNESS DRAUGHT
- 220G DEMERARA SUGAR
- 5ML (1 TEASPOON) BITTER TRUTH JERRY THOMAS BITTERS OR OTHER AROMATIC BITTERS

Pour the Guinness into a saucepan over a medium heat and warm for 10 minutes. Add the sugar and bitters and heat, stirring, to dissolve the sugar. Once dissolved, turn off the heat and allow to cool for 1 hour.

Strain through a fine strainer into a clean bottle. This should keep for 1 week in the fridge.

IRN BRU REDUCTION

Boils off excess water and concentrates the flavour.

- 1 × 330ML CAN OF IRN BRU
- 175G CASTER SUGAR
- 2 DASHES OF BITTERS

Pour the IRN BRU into a saucepan over a medium heat and warm for 10 minutes. Add the sugar and bitters and heat, stirring, to dissolve the sugar. Once dissolved, turn off the heat and allow to cool for 1 hour.

Strain through a fine strainer into a clean bottle. This should keep for 1 week in the fridge.

FOAMS

The theatre of a good foam is a great way to activate a cocktail as it changes both the aesthetic and the texture of the serves. The White Chocolate Foam is used in many of our Alchemist classics. Once you have mastered the basics, you can experiment with a variety of flavours using syrups.

These foams will all keep for 4 days inside a foamer in the fridge, or 2–3 days in an airtight container in the fridge.

GINGER FOAM
MAKES 500ML
- 150ML AQUAFABA
- 150ML GINGER BEER
- 200ML GINGER SYRUP
- YOU WILL ALSO NEED A 500ML FOAMER WITH 1 × N_2O CHARGE (OPTIONAL)

WITH A 500ML FOAMER
Stir all the ingredients together in a jug until well combined, then pour into the foamer. Put on the lid and secure tightly. Charge the foamer with a N_2O charge and shake well before using.

WITHOUT A FOAMER
Stir all the ingredients together in a large mixing bowl until well combined. Use an electric whisk to whip the mixture until it forms stiff peaks. Carefully transfer this mixture into a piping bag with a nozzle and refrigerate until ready to use.

WHITE CHOCOLATE FOAM
MAKES 500ML
- 350ML WHIPPING CREAM
- 50ML WHOLE MILK
- 100ML WHITE CHOCOLATE SYRUP (WE USE GIFFARD)
- YOU WILL ALSO NEED A 500ML FOAMER WITH 1 × N_2O CHARGE (OPTIONAL)

WITH A 500ML FOAMER
Stir all the ingredients together in a jug until well combined, then pour into the foamer. Put on the lid and secure tightly. Charge the foamer with a N_2O charge and shake well before using.

WITHOUT A FOAMER
Stir all the ingredients together in a large mixing bowl until well combined. Use an electric whisk to whip the mixture until it forms stiff peaks. Carefully transfer this mixture into a piping bag with a nozzle and refrigerate until ready to use.

ADVOCAAT FOAM

MAKES 500ML

- 250ML WHIPPING CREAM
- 250ML ADVOCAAT
- YOU WILL ALSO NEED A 500ML FOAMER WITH 1 × N_2O CHARGE (OPTIONAL)

WITH A 500ML FOAMER

Stir all the ingredients together in a jug until well combined, then pour into the foamer. Put on the lid and secure tightly. Charge the foamer with a N_2O charge and shake well before using.

WITHOUT A FOAMER

Stir all the ingredients together in a large mixing bowl until well combined. Use an electric whisk to whip the mixture until it forms stiff peaks. Carefully transfer this mixture into a piping bag with a nozzle and refrigerate until ready to use.

MERINGUE FOAM

MAKES 500ML

- 165ML AQUAFABA
- 165ML VANILLA SYRUP
- 165ML FILTERED WATER
- 1 TEASPOON ULTRATEX POWDER
- YOU WILL ALSO NEED A 500ML FOAMER WITH 1 × N_2O CHARGE (OPTIONAL)

WITH A 500ML FOAMER

Stir all the ingredients together in a jug until well combined, making sure there are no lumps, then pour into the foamer. Put on the lid and secure tightly. Charge the foamer with a N_2O charge and shake well before using. Test the meringue foam before using in a drink: if it doesn't form stiff peaks, then charge again with one more N_2O charge.

WITHOUT A FOAMER

Stir all the ingredients together in a large mixing bowl until well combined, making sure there are no lumps. Use an electric whisk to whip the mixture until it forms stiff peaks. Carefully transfer this mixture into a piping bag with a nozzle and refrigerate until ready to use.

BAILEYS FOAM

MAKES 500ML

- 200ML BAILEYS IRISH CREAM
- 200ML WHIPPING CREAM
- 50ML AQUAFABA
- 50ML WHOLE MILK
- 1G SEA SALT
- YOU WILL ALSO NEED A 500ML FOAMER WITH 1 × N_2O CHARGE (OPTIONAL)

WITH A 500ML FOAMER

Stir all the ingredients together in a jug until well combined, then pour into the foamer. Put on the lid and secure tightly. Charge the foamer with a N_2O charge and shake well before using.

WITHOUT A FOAMER

Stir all the ingredients together in a large

mixing bowl until well combined. Use an electric whisk to whip the mixture until it forms stiff peaks. Carefully transfer this mixture into a piping bag with a nozzle and refrigerate until ready to use.

WATERMELON FOAM
MAKES 450ML
- 150ML AQUAFABA
- 150ML WATERMELON SYRUP
- 150ML CRANBERRY JUICE
- 2 DROPS OF ULTRAFOAM
- YOU WILL ALSO NEED A 500ML FOAMER WITH 1 × N_2O CHARGE (OPTIONAL)

WITH A 500ML FOAMER
Stir all the ingredients together in a jug until well combined, then pour into the foamer. Put on the lid and secure tightly. Charge the foamer with a N_2O charge and shake well before using.

WITHOUT A FOAMER
Stir all the ingredients together in a large mixing bowl until well combined. Use an electric whisk to whip the mixture until it forms stiff peaks. Carefully transfer this mixture into a piping bag with a nozzle and refrigerate until ready to use.

BASIL FOAM
MAKES 500ML
- 150ML AQUAFABA
- 150ML APPLE JUICE
- 150ML BASIL SYRUP
- 50ML SIMPLE SUGAR SYRUP (PAGE 28)
- YOU WILL ALSO NEED A 500ML FOAMER WITH 1 × N_2O CHARGE (OPTIONAL)

WITH A 500ML FOAMER
Stir all the ingredients together in a jug until well combined, then pour into the foamer. Put on the lid and secure tightly. Charge the foamer with a N_2O charge and shake well before using.

WITHOUT A FOAMER
Stir all the ingredients together in a large mixing bowl until well combined. Use an electric whisk to whip the mixture until it forms stiff peaks. Carefully transfer this mixture into a piping bag with a nozzle and refrigerate until ready to use.

HAZELNUT FOAM
MAKES 500ML
- 350ML WHIPPING CREAM
- 50ML WHOLE MILK
- 100ML HAZELNUT SYRUP
- YOU WILL ALSO NEED A 500ML FOAMER WITH 1 × N_2O CHARGE (OPTIONAL)

WITH A 500ML FOAMER
Stir all the ingredients together in a jug until well combined, then pour into the foamer. Put on the lid and secure tightly. Charge the foamer with a N_2O charge and shake well before using.

WITHOUT A FOAMER
Stir all the ingredients together in a large mixing bowl until well combined. Use an electric whisk to whip the mixture until it forms stiff peaks. Carefully transfer this mixture into

a piping bag with a nozzle and refrigerate until
ready to use.

MINT CHOC FOAM
MAKES 450ML
- 300ML MINT CHOC CHIP ICE CREAM
- 150ML WHOLE MILK
- 0.1G GREEN COLOURING POWDER
- YOU WILL ALSO NEED A 500ML FOAMER
  WITH 1 × N_2O CHARGE (OPTIONAL)

WITH A 500ML FOAMER
Allow the ice cream to melt, then strain
to remove the chocolate chips. Stir all the
ingredients together in a jug until well
combined, then pour into the foamer. Put on the
lid and secure tightly. Charge the foamer with
a N_2O charge and shake well before using.

WITHOUT A FOAMER
Allow the ice cream to melt, then strain
to remove the chocolate chips. Stir all the
ingredients together in a large mixing bowl
until well combined. Use an electric whisk
to whip the mixture until it forms stiff peaks.
Carefully transfer this mixture into a piping bag
with a nozzle and refrigerate until ready to use.

COCKTAILS

ARIES

RAM

FIRE SIGN

1ST SIGN OF THE ZODIAC

CARDINAL ENERGY

RULING PLANET IS MARS

Aries is the energetic pioneer of the zodiac, stepping into the spotlight with a vibrant spirit! Ruled by Mars, the planet of action, those born under this sign are often seen as the youngest souls in astrology, brimming with curiosity and a desire to explore. They don't wait around for life to happen; instead, they jump in and make things happen!

As Aries season arrives, it ushers in a fresh wave of energy and excitement, marking the transition from winter to spring. Aries individuals bring passion and a competitive edge to everything they do. When it comes to emotions, they're straightforward and don't shy away from expressing how they feel, diving right into the heart of the matter.

While they might struggle with patience and long-term planning – often craving instant gratification – their boldness and adventurous spirit truly shine. Aries personalities are lively and determined, always ready to take the lead and pursue their goals with enthusiasm!

COCKTAILS

COLOUR-CHANGING ONE

GRAND MARGARITA

GINGER KICK

TAMMY'S MARGARITA

RASPBERRY RIPPLE

NON-ALCOHOLIC

SHADE SWITCHER

COLOUR-CHANGING ONE

VODKA, CITRUS, MAGIC

Aries are fiercely competitive, driven by an innate desire to win and be better, so we created this cocktail because it is hands down one of the best, and a clear winner – just like you. It's also the most infamous cocktail on the menu, where the magic happens before your eyes and you become The Alchemist. For a striking presentation, add dry ice.

MAKES 1 · GLASSWARE: ROCKS

- 25ML VODKA
- 25ML (1 TABLESPOON) GREEN APPLE LIQUEUR
- 15ML (1 TABLESPOON) SIMPLE SUGAR SYRUP (PAGE 28)
- 15ML (1 TABLESPOON) CITRIC ACID DILUTION (PAGE 14)
- 50ML LEMONADE
- 5ML MAGIC MIX (PAGE 16)
- ICE CUBES
- 5–6 PELLETS OF DRY ICE (OPTIONAL), TO SERVE

Add the vodka, apple liqueur, Sugar Syrup and Magic Mix to one glass. Add the Citric Acid Dilution and lemonade to another glass.

Add ice to your rocks glass, then pour the mix from the first glass into the rocks glass. Pour over the lemonade mix and watch the drink as it changes colour.

If you like, place the dry ice pellets on top to serve. Wait for the dry ice to subside before consuming.

GRAND MARGARITA

LIME, CINNAMON, TEQUILA

A Grand Margarita for a grand personality; bigger and better than your average Marg. Aries carry a bold confidence that often makes them bigger and better than everyone else, radiating an infectious energy that inspires others.

MAKES 1 · GLASSWARE: COUPE

- 25ML CINNAMON TEQUILA (PAGE 27)
- 5ML (1 TEASPOON) MEZCAL
- 25ML GRAND MARNIER
- 25ML LIME JUICE
- 15ML (1 TABLESPOON) CINNAMON SYRUP (WE USE GIFFARD)
- ICE CUBES
- GROUND CINNAMON
- GRATED NUTMEG
- CASTER SUGAR
- LIME WEDGE

Add the tequila, mezcal, Grand Marnier, lime juice and cinnamon syrup to a Boston shaker along with the ice and shake for 30 seconds, or until condensation forms on the outside of the shaker.

Prepare a coupe with a cinnamon sugar rim. Mix ground cinnamon and nutmeg with caster sugar on a plate. Rim your coupe with a lime wedge and roll the rim through the sugar mix. Strain the cocktail through a fine strainer into the coupe.

GINGER KICK

GIN, GINGER, FOAM

Aries thrive on adventure, embracing life with a fiery enthusiasm that fuels their daring spirit and compels them to seek out new experiences, challenges and thrills at every turn. This drink will kick-start you into the next exciting adventure.

MAKES 1 · GLASSWARE: HIGHBALL

- ICE CUBES
- 50ML MAKRUT LIME LEAF-INFUSED GIN (PAGE 27)
- 25ML LIME JUICE
- 1 DASH OF BITTER TRUTH JERRY THOMAS BITTERS OR OTHER AROMATIC BITTERS

- 75ML GINGER BEER
- GINGER FOAM (PAGE 32), TO GARNISH
- 3 MAKRUT LIME LEAVES, TO GARNISH

Fill your highball glass with ice cubes, then pour in the gin, lime juice, bitters and ginger beer. Lightly stir to just combine.

Serve, garnished with Ginger Foam and makrut lime leaves.

TAMMY'S MARGARITA

TEQUILA, IRON BRU, DIP

Igniting the flames and revving those engines to full throttle, it's the perfect energy boost every Aries craves to keep their vibrant spirit soaring! This is the fuel to drive you to be the best in every challenge, the winner in every race and keep your unwavering perseverance.

MAKES 1 · GLASSWARE: ROCKS

- 45ML (3 TABLESPOONS) PATRÓN SILVER
- 25ML VELVET FALERNUM
- 25ML LIME JUICE
- 25ML IRN BRU REDUCTION (PAGE 31)
- ICE CUBES
- IRN BRU LOLLIPOP (PAGE 18). TO GARNISH
- LIME SHERBET POWDER. TO GARNISH

Add the Patrón Silver, Velvet Falernum, lime juice and IRN BRU Reduction to a Boston shaker along with the ice and shake for 30 seconds, or until condensation forms on the outside of the shaker.

Add ice cubes to a rocks glass and strain in the cocktail through a fine strainer. Garnish with an IRN BRU Lollipop and Sherbet.

SHADE SWITCHER

APPLE, CITRUS, MAGIC

Aries thrive on excitement and are always ready to embrace the next adventure, fuelled by their passion for change and movement. This cocktail embodies that spirit of spontaneity, making it a true standout that matches your vibrant energy.

MAKES 1 · GLASSWARE: ROCKS

- 25ML FILTERED WATER
- 15ML (1 TABLESPOON) SIMPLE SUGAR SYRUP (PAGE 28)
- 5ML (1 TEASPOON) MAGIC MIX (PAGE 16)
- 1ML APPLE FLAVOUR DROPS

- 15ML (1 TABLESPOON) CITRIC ACID DILUTION (PAGE 14)
- 50ML LEMONADE
- ICE CUBES
- DISCO LOLLY (PAGE 18), TO GARNISH

Add the water, Sugar Syrup and Magic Mix to one glass and the Citric Acid dilution, lemonade and apple flavour drops to another glass.

Add the ice cubes to your rocks glass, then pour over the mix from the first glass. Pour over the lemonade mix and watch the drink as it changes colour.

Serve, garnished with a Disco Lolly.

RASPBERRY RIPPLE

RASPBERRY, GIN, FIZZ

Driven by your dynamic nature and fearless ambition, you love to make ripples in the world and leave a lasting impact wherever you go.

MAKES 1 · GLASSWARE: FLUTE

- 15ML (1 TABLESPOON) WHITLEY NEILL RASPBERRY GIN
- 15ML (1 TABLESPOON) LICOR 43
- 15ML (1 TABLESPOON) RASPBERRY LIQUEUR
- 15ML (1 TABLESPOON) CITRIC ACID DILUTION (PAGE 14)
- 10ML (2 TEASPOONS) RASPBERRY SYRUP
- 1 DROP OF ULTRAFOAM
- ICE CUBES
- 50ML PROSECCO

Add all the ingredients except the prosecco and ice to a Boston shaker. Add the ice cubes to a Boston glass, pop the Boston tin part on top of glass and shake for 30 seconds. Remove the Boston glass and pour the liquid into a flute, using a Hawthorne and fine strainer.

Top with the prosecco and serve.

TAURUS

BULL

EARTH SIGN

2ND SIGN OF THE ZODIAC

FIXED ENERGY

RULING PLANET IS VENUS

Taurus is the grounded lover of the zodiac, embracing life through their senses! Ruled by Venus — the planet of beauty and pleasure — those born under this sign have an incredible appreciation for the finer things in life. They thrive on home comforts and have a special love for delicious food, savouring every bite with an amazing sense of smell, truly living life through their senses.

Safety and security are their top priorities, and they create cosy havens that reflect their taste and style. Taurus prefer stability and routine, finding comfort in the familiar and resisting change whenever and wherever possible. They avoid changing their jobs, friendships and partnerships at all costs.

Taurus are powerful, strong and resilient, both mentally and physically, and emotionally they are the most grounded in the zodiac. With their affectionate nature, Taurus are incredibly loving, romantic and fiercely loyal, showing love through kind gestures and patience. They love to be outside in nature, and as Taurus season unfolds, it brings a sense of tranquillity and richness, celebrating the abundance of spring.

COCKTAILS

THE TRIFLE

CHERRY POPPINS

SIDE OF CAVIAR

THE EDIBLE ONE

FRENCH KISS

NON-ALCOHOLIC

FRUBE

THE TRIFLE

BOOZY, JELLY, CREAM

Taurus have a particular fondness for desserts, relishing the sweet indulgence of treats that tantalise their taste buds and bring them pure bliss with every delectable bite. We hope this cocktail hits the spot.

MAKES 1 · GLASSWARE: TUBO
YOU WILL ALSO NEED A SPOON

- 25ML VODKA
- 25ML APEROL
- 50ML APPLE JUICE
- 25ML STRAWBERRY PURÉE
- ICE CUBES

- 1 SERVING OF STRAWBERRY JELLY (PAGE 17), TO SERVE
- ADVOCAAT FOAM (PAGE 33), TO GARNISH
- SPRINKLES, TO GARNISH

Add the vodka, Aperol, apple juice and strawberry purée to a Boston shaker with some ice and shake for 30 seconds, or until condensation forms on the outside of the shaker.

Remove your jelly in its glass from the fridge. Strain the cocktail through a fine strainer over the jelly, then garnish with the Advocaat Foam and sprinkles. Serve with a spoon.

CHERRY POPPINS

GIN, CHERRY, POP

Taurus possess a refined sense of smell and taste, immersing themselves in life's pleasures and experiences as they navigate the world through their heightened senses, savouring every moment to the fullest.

MAKES 1 · GLASSWARE: NICK & NORA, CHILLED
YOU WILL ALSO NEED A FLAVOUR BLASTER

- 15ML (1 TABLESPOON) RASPBERRY GIN
- 15ML (1 TABLESPOON) AMARETTO
- 15ML (1 TABLESPOON) CHERRY LIQUEUR
- 25ML CITRIC ACID DILUTION (PAGE 14)
- 50ML CRANBERRY JUICE
- 15ML (1 TABLESPOON) STRAWBERRY SYRUP
- ICE CUBES

Pour all the ingredients into a Boston shaker, add some ice and stir for 30 seconds or until condensation forms on the outside of the shaker.

Strain into the chilled glass. Use a Flavour Blaster to add a bubble on top of the drink, then serve.

SIDE OF CAVIAR

COINTREAU, COGNAC, CAVIAR

Ruled by Venus, Taurus have a profound love for the finer things in life, embracing beauty, luxury and indulgence in both their surroundings and experiences, making them true connoisseurs of comfort and elegance.

MAKES 1 · GLASSWARE: NICK & NORA

- 50ML HENNESSY VS COGNAC
- 15ML (1 TABLESPOON) COINTREAU
- 22.5ML LEMON JUICE
- 2 BAR SPOONS ALCHEMIST MARMALADE (PAGE 16)
- GRAPEFRUIT ZEST
- ICE CUBES
- 1 TEASPOON PASSIONFRUIT CAVIAR, TO GARNISH

Add all ingredients, except the Caviar, to a Boston glass with some ice cubes. Stir the drink using a cocktail spoon for 30 seconds, then pour the drink through a fine strainer into a Nick and Nora glass.

Garnish with some Caviar and serve.

THE EDIBLE ONE

APPLE, CHOCOLATE, WAFER

Taurus have a deep appreciation for food, relishing every bite and often indulging in culinary experiences that delight their senses and celebrate the pleasures of life, so of course we created an edible drink just for you.

MAKES 1 · GLASSWARE: WAFER CUP (WE USE STROODLES)

- 25ML GREEN APPLE LIQUEUR
- 15ML (1 TABLESPOON) CALVADOS
- 10ML (2 TEASPOONS) BRISTOL SYRUP COMPANY LIME SHERBET
- 10ML (2 TEASPOONS) SALTED CARAMEL SYRUP
- 50ML APPLE JUICE
- 25ML WHITE CHOCOLATE FOAM (PAGE 32), PLUS MORE TO GARNISH
- ICE CUBES
- 1 WAFER CUP
- GROUND CINNAMON, TO GARNISH
- GROUND NUTMEG, TO GARNISH

Add the green apple liqueur, Calvados, Lime Sherbet, salted caramel syrup and apple juice to a Boston shaker, along with 25ml of White Chocolate Foam. Add some ice cubes and shake for 30 seconds.

Using a fine strainer, pour the liquid into a wafer cup.

Garnish the drink with more White Chocolate Foam and a light dusting of cinnamon and nutmeg.

FRENCH KISS

VODKA, BERRIES, CRACKLE

Taurus express love so deeply, making your partners feel so cherished and adored – behind closed doors of course, as we know you hate a PDA. So this is the perfect drink for the most romantic and loving souls in the zodiac.

MAKES 1 · GLASSWARE: COUPE

- 25ML VODKA
- 25ML RASPBERRY SYRUP
- 15ML (1 TABLESPOON) MOUSE
  KINGDOM DARK BERRIES LIQUEUR
- 25ML PINEAPPLE JUICE
- 25ML CRANBERRY JUICE

- 5ML (1 TEASPOON) LEMON MIX (PAGE 14)
- ICE CUBES
- MERINGUE FOAM (PAGE 33),
  TO GARNISH
- SILICONE TONGUE, TO GARNISH
- CRACKLING CANDY, TO GARNISH

Add the vodka, raspberry syrup, berry liqueur, pineapple and cranberry juices and Lemon Mix to a Boston shaker along with some ice cubes and stir for 30 seconds, or until condensation forms on the outside of the shaker.

Strain the cocktail through a fine strainer into a coupe glass, then garnish with Meringue Foam and top with a silicone tongue and crackling candy.

FRUBE

VANILLA, STRAWBERRY, DREAM

Food flavours – what's not to love? With your deep appreciation for food, we made you another drink for your finely tuned taste buds.

MAKES 1 · GLASSWARE: HIGHBALL

- 50ML APPLE JUICE
- 50ML ORANGE JUICE
- 15ML (1 TABLESPOON) LEMON MIX (PAGE 14)
- 10ML (2 TEASPOONS) STRAWBERRY SHRUB SYRUP
- 10ML (2 TEASPOONS) CHERRY AND VANILLA SYRUP
- 50ML WHITE CHOCOLATE FOAM (PAGE 22)
- ICE CUBES
- 2 DEHYDRATED STRAWBERRY SLICES (PAGE 24), TO GARNISH

Add the apple and orange juices, Lemon Mix, both syrups and the White Chocolate Foam to a Boston shaker along with some ice cubes and shake for 30 seconds, or until condensation forms on the outside of the shaker.

Add ice cubes to your glass, then strain in the cocktail through a fine strainer. Serve garnished with the Dehydrated Strawberry slices.

GEMINI

TWINS

AIR SIGN

3RD SIGN OF THE ZODIAC

MUTABLE ENERGY

RULING PLANET IS MERCURY

Gemini is the curious communicator of the zodiac, bursting with energy and ideas that spark vibrant conversations! Ruled by Mercury, the planet of communication, those born under this sign are often seen as the social butterflies of astrology; they are the forever learners on their quest for knowledge and growth. They love to organise family and social meet-ups, taking the lead and managing everyone, ensuring they are happy and included.

As Gemini season arrives, it ushers in a lively atmosphere filled with fun. Gemini individuals bring wit and charm to every interaction. Emotionally, they embrace their dual nature, often balancing logic with feelings in a playful dance.

They are adaptable creatures, constantly seeking a change of scenery and love to organise short trips, learning and exploring as they go. They are great at multitasking, have a finger in every pie, are curious to a fault and are generally well informed and up to date on all the gossip and latest news.

Nervousness and worry are common traits with this zodiac placement. Underlying restlessness mean Geminis need more stimulation than others. They usually read, talk and think a lot, with an airy, mutable energy, and are at their best when they have plenty of things to do.

COCKTAILS

PEAR-PLE RAIN

TONGUE-TIED MAI TAI

BANANA SPLIT

WOO LAGOON

THE IRISH

NON-ALCOHOLIC

ITALIAN SPRITZ

PEAR-PLE RAIN

PEAR, HONEY, RAIN

Did you know Prince was a Gemini? You can use that fun fact when you meet new people – and we know how much you love to chat to new people! Geminis have an insatiable passion for chatting, effortlessly engaging in lively conversations that spark curiosity and connection.

MAKES 1 · GLASSWARE: TEST TUBE OR HIGHBALL

- 25ML PEAR LIQUEUR
- 25ML HONEY SYRUP (PAGE 28)
- 75ML PROSECCO
- ICE CUBES

- INDIGO DROPS (PAGE 21), TO GARNISH
- 2 PELLETS DRY ICE, TO GARNISH

Add the pear liqueur, Honey Syrup and prosecco to a Boston shaker along with some ice cubes and stir for 30 seconds, or until condensation forms on the outside of the shaker.

Strain the cocktail through a fine strainer into your glass. To garnish, add a few drops of Indigo Drops, with a syringe and a couple of pellets of dry ice on top of the drink. Serve.

TONGUE-TIED MAI TAI

RUM, SHERBET, AIR

We're pretty sure it's unlikely you will ever be tongue-tied, but you never know ... With your quick thinking and sharp sense of humour, Geminis can effortlessly lighten the mood with your banter and playful charm.

MAKES 1 · GLASSWARE: ROCKS
YOU WILL ALSO NEED AN AIR MACHINE

- 25ML DARK RUM
- 15ML (1 TABLESPOON) DISCARDED BANANA PEEL RUM
- 5ML (1 TEASPOON) WRAY & NEPHEW OVERPROOF RUM
- 15ML (1 TABLESPOON) ALMOND SYRUP
- 5ML (1 TEASPOON) GRENADINE SYRUP
- 25ML LIME JUICE
- ICE CUBES
- LIME SHERBET AIR (PAGE 18), TO GARNISH

Add all the rums, almond and grenadine syrups and lime juice to a Boston shaker along with some ice cubes and shake for 30 seconds, or until condensation forms on the outside of the shaker.

Add some ice cubes to your rocks glass, then strain in the cocktail through a fine strainer.

To garnish, have your air machine turned on and add your Lime Sherbet Air. Once ready, spoon the air onto the cocktail, leaving a good layer on top of your drink.

BANANA SPLIT

CHOCOLATE, MILK, DECADENCE

Geminis are known for their split personality, seamlessly embodying dual aspects of themselves – one moment playful and sociable, the next introspective and contemplative – making them wonderfully complex and intriguing individuals.

MAKES 1 · GLASSWARE: EDIBLE CUP

- 25ML DISCARDED BANANA PEEL RUM
- 15ML (1 TABLESPOON) BANANA LIQUEUR
- 10ML (2 TEASPOONS) STRAWBERRY PURÉE
- 75ML TONY'S CHOCOLATE MILK (PAGE 16)

- PINCH OF SEA SALT
- ICE CUBES
- WHITE CHOCOLATE FOAM (PAGE 32), TO GARNISH
- 1 MARASCHINO CHERRY, TO GARNISH
- GOLD CHOCOLATE BANANA (PAGE 22), TO GARNISH

Add the banana rum, liqueur, strawberry purée, Chocolate Milk and sea salt to a Boston shaker along with some ice cubes and shake for 30 seconds, or until condensation forms on the outside of the shaker.

Strain the cocktail through a fine strainer into your edible cup and garnish with White Chocolate Foam. Top the foam with a cherry and your Chocolate Banana.

WOO LAGOON

VODKA, RASPBERRY, SHIMMER

You easily woo people with your tantalising chat and natural charm, using your quick wit and engaging conversation skills to connect with anyone you meet, thus making social interactions feel effortless and enjoyable.

MAKES 1 · GLASSWARE: COLLINS

- 25ML VODKA
- 25ML RASPBERRY LIQUEUR
- 50ML CITRIC ACID DILUTION (PAGE 14)
- 50ML RASPBERRY SYRUP
- 200ML SODA WATER
- 0.4G BLUE COLOURING POWDER
- 1G SILVER METALLIC POWDER
- ICE CUBES

Add the vodka, liqueur, Citric Acid Dilution, raspberry syrup, soda water and coloured powders to a mixing jug. Stir to mix in the powders and liquid.

Add some ice to a collins glass, then pour in the cocktail. Serve.

THE IRISH

WHISKEY, ESPRESSO, BAILEYS

Geminis hate to get bored and always yearn for a change of scenery, so they love to travel and meet new people in far-flung places. This warming drink might tempt you to organise your next trip.

MAKES 1 · GLASSWARE: HANDLED HEATPROOF

- 45ML (3 TABLESPOONS) IRISH WHISKEY
- 15ML (1 TABLESPOON) DEMERARA SYRUP
- BOILING WATER
- 1 SHOT OF ESPRESSO
- BAILEYS FOAM (PAGE 33), TO GARNISH
- GROUND CINNAMON, TO GARNISH
- GRATED NUTMEG, TO GARNISH

Add the whiskey and syrup to your handled heatproof glass. Top with a good amount of boiling water, but leave enough room to add your espresso. Lightly stir in the espresso.

Garnish with Baileys Foam and a light dusting of cinnamon and nutmeg.

ITALIAN SPRITZ

SPRITZY, CITRUS, TONIC

The perfect companion for reminiscing about sun-soaked getaways with friends! Sip and savour as you drift back to your happiest memories, exploring vibrant streets and embracing every moment of your intricately planned mini-adventures. Cheers to laughter, holidays and the joy of travel!

MAKES 1 · GLASSWARE: WINE

- ICE CUBES
- 50ML LYRE'S ITALIAN SPRITZ
- 25ML CITRIC ACID DILUTION (PAGE 14)

- 100ML TONIC WATER
- ORANGE WEDGE, TO GARNISH

Add some ice cubes to your glass, then pour in all the ingredients and gently stir. Serve garnished with an orange wedge.

CANCER

CRAB

WATER SIGN

4TH SIGN OF THE ZODIAC

CARDINAL ENERGY

RULING PLANET IS THE MOON

Cancer is the intuitive caregiver of the zodiac, looking after others with compassion and empathy. Ruled by the moon, the planet of emotions, those born under this sign possess a sensitivity that allows them to connect deeply with the feelings of others. They create close relationships with unwavering dedication and compassion. As Cancer season unfolds, it brings a wave of introspection, celebrating the bonds of family and home, as they love to nurture the people nearest and dearest to them.

Cancer individuals approach life with a protective instinct, fiercely loyal to their loved ones and always ready to lend a listening ear. When it comes to love, they are nurturing and heartfelt, expressing their emotions in tender and meaningful ways. However, nothing is crabbier than the crab, so watch out when they snap! Cancers need lots of alone time to feel and embrace their emotions, and to soothe themselves and heal, so keep your distance.

While they may sometimes retreat into their shells when feeling vulnerable, their intuition and caring nature truly shine. Cancers love to collect memorabilia and reminders of all the places they visit, and they hold onto these trinkets and keepsakes. Some may call it clutter, but for them it's memories.

COCKTAILS

COSMIC OYSTER

BATTERNBERG

FOAM ALONE

THE EGG

BASIL SMASH

NON-ALCOHOLIC

COS NO

COSMIC OYSTER

DECADENT, LIQUID, MORSEL

These sensitive souls are heavily affected by the moon, and when the world becomes too much they retreat into their shells. They are deeply intuitive and embody a celestial connection that allows them to sense the emotions of others.

MAKES 24 (PERFECT FOR A SOIRÉE)
YOU WILL NEED OYSTER SHELLS

- 150ML BOMBAY CITRON PRESSÉ
- 50ML LIMONCELLO
- 100ML WATER
- 100ML CITRIC ACID DILUTION (PAGE 14)
- 150ML MONIN YUZU PURÉE
- 50ML BRISTOL SYRUP COMPANY DISCO BLUE
- CRUSHED ICE
- PASSIONFRUIT CAVIAR, TO GARNISH

Add all ingredients bar the Passionfruit Caviar to a large mixing jug and stir to combine.

Cover a lipped serving dish with a good layer of crushed ice, then place the oyster shells evenly around the ice, ensuring they're level.

Portion 25ml of your Cosmic Oyster liquid into the shells. Garnish with a teaspoon of Passionfruit Caviar. Any leftover Cosmic Oyster liquid will keep in the fridge for 1 week.

BATTENBERG

RUM, ALMOND, AIR

In traditional astrology, Cancer rules the 4th house of the home and family. Their nurturing nature shines in the kitchen in particular, where they express their love through thoughtful gestures like baking cakes and whipping up other delicious treats, pouring their heart into every recipe.

MAKES 1 · GLASSWARE: ROCKS
YOU WILL ALSO NEED AN AIR MACHINE

- 25ML DARK RUM
- 15ML (1 TABLESPOON) WRAY & NEPHEW OVERPROOF RUM
- 15ML (1 TABLESPOON) LIME JUICE
- 25ML ORANGE JUICE
- 25ML PINEAPPLE JUICE
- 25ML PASSIONFRUIT SYRUP
- 5ML (1 TEASPOON) GRENADINE SYRUP
- ICE CUBES
- BATTENBERG AIR (PAGE 21), TO GARNISH

Add both the rums, all the fruit juices and the syrups to a Boston shaker along with some ice cubes and shake for 30 seconds, or until condensation forms on the outside of the shaker.

Add ice cubes to a rocks glass, then strain in the cocktail through a fine strainer.

To garnish, have your air machine turned on and add in your Battenberg Air. Once ready, spoon the air onto the cocktail in your rocks glass in a good layer.

FOAM ALONE

GIN, APEROL, FOAMY

Cancers love alone time, and there is nothing more indulgent that hanging around indoors with no plan. Cancers cherish the comfort and security of home, often viewing it as their sanctuary, somewhere they can retreat to recharge and express their nurturing nature. They take great pride in creating a warm, inviting atmosphere filled with personal touches, cosy decor and cherished memories, making their home a reflection of their emotions and values.

MAKES 1 · GLASSWARE: COUPE

- 25ML GIN
- 15ML (1 TABLESPOON) APEROL
- 5ML (1 TEASPOON) VIOLETTE LIQUEUR, (WE USE GIFFARD)
- 25ML CITRIC ACID DILUTION (PAGE 14)
- 15ML (1 TABLESPOON) BLUEBERRY PURÉE
- 10ML (2 TEASPOONS) SIMPLE SUGAR SYRUP (PAGE 28)
- 3 DROPS OF ULTRAFOAM
- 0.1G METALLIC SILVER POWDER
- ICE CUBES
- 2 PELLETS OF DRY ICE
- 50ML LEMONADE

Add the gin, Aperol, liqueur, Citric Acid Dilution, blueberry purée, sugar syrup, UltraFoam and silver powder to a Boston shaker along with some ice cubes and shake for 30 seconds, or until condensation forms on the outside of the shaker.

Muddle a couple of pellets of dry ice in the bottom of your coupe glass.

Add the lemonade to the shaker, stir to combine then strain the cocktail through a fine strainer into the coupe glass. Wait for the dry ice to subside before consuming.

THE EGG

ELDERFLOWER, CITRUS, CUCUMBER

Cancers are amazing nurturers, embodying a deep sense of empathy and care that extends to people, animals and even their environments. Their instinctive ability to sense the needs of others allows them to provide emotional support and comfort, making them trusted confidants and loving friends. Take time to nurture yourself – for once – and enjoy this uplifting cocktail.

MAKES 1 · GLASSWARE: WE USE A PORCELAIN EGG, BE AS ADVENTUROUS AS POSSIBLE YOU WILL ALSO NEED A STRAW

- ICE CUBES
- 45ML (3 TABLESPOONS) HENDRICK'S GIN
- 15ML (1 TABLESPOON) ST-GERMAIN ELDERFLOWER LIQUEUR
- 15ML (1 TABLESPOON) LEMON MIX (PAGE 14)
- 25ML MONIN YUZU PURÉE
- 1 × 250ML CAN OF PUNCHY CUCUMBER, YUZU & ROSEMARY
- 2 PELLETS OF DRY ICE, TO GARNISH

Fill your glass with ice cubes and add all the other ingredients, except the dry ice. Gently stir together.

Place the dry ice pellets on top of the drink and add a straw. Wait for the dry ice to subside before consuming.

BASIL SMASH

BASIL, PEACH, SMASH

Cancers can be moody, as their deep emotional currents often ebb and flow, leading to moments of vulnerability and intensity. When overwhelmed by their feelings, they may feel the urge to lash out or express their frustration in physical ways, which can occasionally result in smashing things in a fit of passion or anger. So this drink is the perfect solution to venting that frustration!

MAKES 1 · GLASSWARE: TUBO
YOU WILL ALSO NEED A SPOON

- 50ML GIN
- 15ML (1 TABLESPOON) LIME JUICE
- 15ML (1 TABLESPOON) PEACH
  LIQUEUR
- 10ML (2 TEASPOONS) BASIL SYRUP

- 8 BASIL LEAVES
- ICE CUBES
- BASIL GLASS DISC (PAGE 21),
  TO GARNISH

Add the gin, lime juice, peach liqueur, basil syrup and leaves to a Boston shaker with some ice cubes and shake for 30 seconds, or until condensation forms on the outside of the shaker.

Strain the cocktail through a fine strainer into a tubo glass, then serve garnished with a Basil Glass disc and a spoon. Smash the Basil Glass.

COS NO

CITRUS, CRANBERRY, AIR

Cancers possess a keen ability to say no to plans when they sense the need to preserve their energy, prioritising their emotional wellbeing and finding solace in the familiar comforts of home.

MAKES 1 · GLASSWARE: COUPE

- 25ML (1 TABLESPOON) LYRE'S ITALIAN SPRITZ
- 25ML (1 TABLESPOON) EVERLEAF FOREST
- 10ML (2 TEASPOONS) SIMPLE SUGAR SYRUP (PAGE 28)
- 50ML CRANBERRY JUICE
- 5ML (1 TEASPOON) LIME JUICE
- ICE CUBES
- LIME SHERBET AIR (PAGE 18), TO GARNISH

Add the spritz, Everleaf Forest, Sugar Syrup, cranberry and lime juices to a Boston shaker along with some ice cubes and shake for 30 seconds, or until condensation forms on the outside of the shaker.

Strain the cocktail through a fine strainer into a coupe glass, then serve garnished with Lime Sherbet Air.

LEO

LION

FIRE SIGN

5TH SIGN OF THE ZODIAC

FIXED ENERGY

RULING PLANET IS THE SUN

Leo is the radiant social star of the zodiac, shining brightly with charisma and confidence! Ruled by the sun, the source of energy and vitality, those born under this sign exude a magnetic presence that draws others in and inspires admiration. They thrive on fun, creativity and self-expression, often stepping into the spotlight with flair and enthusiasm.

As Leo season arrives, it ignites a spark of passion and creativity, celebrating individuality and self-confidence. Leo individuals approach life with a bold heart, eager to share their talents and spread joy wherever they go, dressing to impress and always having fabulous hair. Truly solar-powered, they love to lie in the sun to recharge their batteries.

Their love is deep and felt from the heart, with a craving for tactile affection, hugs and adoration. They are generous and affectionate, showering their partners with warmth and adoration. While they may sometimes seek validation and struggle with pride, their vibrant spirit and loyalty truly shine. Leo personalities are dynamic and creative, always ready to uplift and inspire those around them with their boundless energy.

COCKTAILS

NEW PORNSTAR

POPSICLE

BIG BABY GUINNESS

CHEEKY VIMTO

DISCO SOUR

NON-ALCOHOLIC

VIRGIN PORNSTAR

NEW PORNSTAR

VODKA, PASSIONFRUIT, FIZZ

In traditional astrology the 5th house is all about fun and sex, and Leos find new ways to have both. Leo is considered the sexiest sign in the zodiac, as they exude a magnetic allure that captures the attention of everyone around them.

MAKES 1 · GLASSWARE: COUPE AND A SHOT

- 25ML VODKA
- 100ML PINEAPPLE JUICE
- 25ML PORNSTAR BATCH (PAGE 16)
- 25ML PASSIONFRUIT SYRUP
- ICE CUBES
- 25ML PROSECCO
- 1 TEASPOON PASSIONFRUIT CAVIAR, TO GARNISH

Add the vodka, pineapple juice, Pornstar Batch and passionfruit syrup to a Boston shaker along with some ice cubes and shake for 30 seconds, or until condensation forms on the outside of the shaker.

Strain the cocktail through a fine strainer into a coupe glass.

Pour prosecco into a shot glass on the side, garnish with the Passionfruit Caviar and serve alongside the New Pornstar.

POPSICLE

PASSIONFRUIT, ORANGE, POP

A fun drink for the big kid within every Leo that likes to play and keep their inner fun alive. Leos have a knack of turning ordinary moments into unforgettable experiences.

**MAKES 1 · GLASSWARE: CONE
YOU WILL ALSO NEED A FLAVOUR BLASTER**

- 25ML TEQUILA
- 5ML (1 TEASPOON) PASSOÃ
- 5ML (1 TEASPOON) COINTREAU
- 25ML LIME JUICE

- 25ML ORANGE JUICE
- 15ML (1 TABLESPOON) MANGO SYRUP
- 5ML (1 TEASPOON) WATER
- ICE CUBES

Add all the ingredients to a Boston shaker including some ice cubes and stir for 30 seconds, or until condensation forms on the outside of the shaker.

Strain the cocktail through a fine strainer into your glass.

Using your Flavour Blaster, add a bubble to garnish this drink, then serve immediately.

BIG BABY GUINNESS

VODKA, COLD BREW, BAILEYS

Why have a Baby Guinness when you can go BIG or go home? Leos love to party; they embody high energy and it's contagious, so they keep the fun and the party alive from dusk until dawn.

MAKES 1 · GLASSWARE: TUBO

- 25ML VODKA
- 25ML GUINNESS REDUCTION (PAGE 32)
- 25ML COLD BREW COFFEE (PAGE 28)
- ICE CUBES
- BAILEYS FOAM (PAGE 33), TO GARNISH

Add the vodka, Guinness Reduction and Coffee to a Boston shaker along with some ice cubes and stir for 30 seconds, or until condensation forms on the outside of the shaker.

Strain the cocktail through a fine strainer into your glass and garnish with Baileys Foam.

CHEEKY VIMTO

GIN, BLOOD ORANGE, VIMTO

Leos are always ready to add a playful twist to any situation. With their infectious sense of humour and mischievous charm, they love to keep things lighthearted and fun.

MAKES 1 · GLASSWARE: BEAKER

- ICE CUBES
- 25ML SLOE GIN
- 15ML (1 TABLESPOON) WHITLEY NEILL BLOOD ORANGE GIN
- 15ML (1 TABLESPOON) LEMON MIX (PAGE 14)

- 25ML VIMTO SQUASH
- 50ML SODA WATER
- 5 ML (1 TEASPOON) CHERRY AND VANILLA SYRUP
- 1 SERVING OF VIMTO JELLY (PAGE 21), TO GARNISH

Add some ice cubes to your glass, then pour in all the ingredients, and lightly stir to mix.

Serve with your Vimto Jelly on the side.

DISCO SOUR

COGNAC, VERMOUTH, SOUR

Leos are the life of the party at discos, radiating confidence and charisma – they are ruled by the sun, after all. You will find them on the dancefloor drawing everyone's attention with their infectious enthusiasm and great dance moves.

MAKES 1 · GLASSWARE: WE USE A CONVECTION GLASS BUT A ROCKS GLASS WOULD WORK WELL

- 45ML (3 TABLESPOONS) COGNAC
- 25M EL BANDARRA AL FRESCO
- 15ML (1 TABLESPOON) BRISTOL SYRUP COMPANY DISCO GRENADINE
- 15ML (1 TABLESPOON) LEMON MIX (PAGE 14)
- 15ML (1 TABLESPOON) BLUEBERRY PURÉE
- 1 DASH OF PEYCHAUD'S BITTERS
- ICE CUBES
- 1 PELLET OF DRY ICE, TO GARNISH

Add all the ingredients except the dry ice to a Boston shaker, including some ice cubes, and stir for 30 seconds, or until condensation forms on the outside of the shaker.

Strain the cocktail through a fine strainer into your glass and garnish with 1 pellet of dry ice. Wait for the dry ice to subside before drinking.

VIRGIN PORNSTAR
PINEAPPLE, PASSION, LEMONADE

Leos are renowned for their creativity in finding fun and romance. With their magnetic charm, they are the sexiest sign in the zodiac. With their bold confidence and magnetic allure, they are often seen as the most likely candidates for the spotlight of a pornstar, effortlessly captivating everyone around them.

MAKES 1 · GLASSWARE: COUPE AND A FLUTE
YOU WILL ALSO NEED A SPOON

- 100ML PINEAPPLE JUICE
- 15ML (1 TABLESPOON) LEMON MIX (PAGE 14)
- 10ML (2 TEASPOONS) VANILLA SYRUP
- 10ML (2 TEASPOONS) PASSIONFRUIT SYRUP

- ICE CUBES
- 25ML LEMONADE
- 1 BAR SPOON PASSIONFRUIT CAVIAR, TO GARNISH

Add the pineapple juice, Lemon Mix and vanilla and passionfruit syrups to a Boston shaker with some ice cubes and hard shake for 30 seconds, or until condensation forms on the outside of the shaker.

Strain the cocktail through a fine strainer into your coupe glass. Pour the lemonade into a flute glass and serve on the side, garnished with a spoon of passionfruit caviar.

VIRGO

MAIDEN

EARTH SIGN

6TH SIGN OF THE ZODIAC

MUTABLE ENERGY

RULING PLANET IS MERCURY

Virgo is the meticulous planner of the zodiac, embodying a practical approach to life that values order, and they really do the detail. Ruled by Mercury, the planet of communication, they have a keen analytical mind and are always efficient. They thrive on organisation and precision, often applying their skills to improve the world around them. You will always call a Virgo to come round if you need help to get things done.

As Virgo season unfolds, it brings a sense of clarity and focus, celebrating the beauty of diligence and hard work. Virgo individuals approach life with a critical eye, always seeking ways to refine and enhance their surroundings. When it comes to love, they are thoughtful and caring, expressing their devotion through acts of service and support.

Natural caregivers, they are great caretakers of plants and animals. While they struggle with perfectionism and self-criticism, their dedication and reliability will truly shine. They are grounded and insightful, always ready to lend a helping hand and bring order to chaos.

COCKTAILS

BUGGED OUT
STRAWBERRY SHRUB BELLINI
BRILL
LAVENDAIR
BREAKING & EGGS

NON-ALCOHOLIC

THE ANTIDOTE

BUGGED OUT

GIN, MELON, FOAM

Virgos love taking care of their bodies and often focus on healthy habits. They have a great eye for detail and pay attention to what they eat and how they exercise. Being in nature makes them happy, as they enjoy the beauty and peace it brings.

MAKES 1 · GLASSWARE: COUPE

- 15ML (1 TABLESPOON) GIN
- 15ML (1 TABLESPOON) MELON LIQUEUR
- 15ML (1 TABLESPOON) BANANA LIQUEUR
- 15ML (1 TABLESPOON) LIME JUICE
- 50ML PINEAPPLE JUICE
- 10ML (2 TEASPOONS) PINEAPPLE AND COCONUT SYRUP
- ICE CUBES
- WATERMELON FOAM (PAGE 34), TO GARNISH

Add all the ingredients to a Boston shaker including some ice cubes and shake for 30 seconds. Pour the liquid into a coupe glass using a fine strainer.

Serve garnished with Watermelon Foam.

STRAWBERRY SHRUB BELLINI

STRAWBERRY, SHRUB, FIZZ

Virgos are the earthly caretakers of the zodiac when it comes to plants and botanicals, as they have such a nurturing spirit. They appreciate the calming effects that plants have on their environment.

MAKES 1 · GLASSWARE: FLUTE

- 25ML MOUSE KINGDOM STRAWBERRY LIQUEUR
- 25ML WHITLEY NEILL RASPBERRY GIN
- 15ML (1 TABLESPOON) CITRIC ACID DILUTION (PAGE 14)
- 10ML (2 TEASPOONS) STRAWBERRY SHRUB SYRUP
- 1 DASH OF ULTRAFOAM
- ICE CUBES
- 30ML PROSECCO

Add all the ingredients, except the prosecco, to a Boston shaker including some ice cubes and shake for 30 seconds, or until condensation forms on the outside of the shaker.

Strain the cocktail through a fine strainer into a flute. Top up with prosecco and serve.

BRILL

RASPBERRY, WHITE CHOCOLATE, SPRINKLES

Virgos are just brilliant — fact. Sometimes they need
a gentle reminder as a show of gratitude for all they do for
everyone else.

MAKES 1 · GLASSWARE: ROCKS

- 25ML LICOR 43
- 25ML RASPBERRY VODKA
- 15ML (1 TABLESPOON) RASPBERRY
  SYRUP
- 50ML CRANBERRY JUICE
- 10ML (2 TEASPOONS) STRAWBERRY
  PURÉE

- ICE CUBES
- CHOCOLATE SAUCE, TO GARNISH
- SPRINKLES, TO GARNISH
- WHITE CHOCOLATE FOAM (PAGE 32),
  TO GARNISH

Add the Licor 43, vodka, raspberry syrup, cranberry juice and strawberry purée
to a Boston shaker along with some ice cubes and shake for 30 seconds, or until
condensation forms on the outside of the shaker.

Prepare a glass with a light rim of chocolate sauce — you can use a pastry brush
for ease. Then coat the rim in sprinkles.

Fill the glass with ice cubes and strain in the cocktail through a fine strainer.

Serve garnished with a dome of White Chocolate Foam.

LAVENDAIR

GIN, LAVENDER, CLOUD

With an air of elegance and twist of herbs to help keep them grounded, this drink will bring Virgos back to their roots as an earth sign.

MAKES 1 · GLASSWARE: COUPE

- 15ML (1 TABLESPOON) TANQUERAY
- 30ML MARTINI RISERVA SPECIALE AMBRATO VERMOUTH OR OTHER WHITE VERMOUTH
- 22.5ML LIME JUICE
- 15ML (1 TABLESPOON) GIFFARD CRÈME DE VIOLETTE
- 7.5ML BLUE CURAÇAO
- ICE CUBES
- LAVENDER AIR (PAGE 24)

Add all the ingredients to a Boston glass. Fill the glass with ice cubes and shake with the Boston tin.

Strain the cocktail through a fine strainer into a coupe glass and top with Lavender Air.

BREAKING & EGGS

SCOTCH, BREAKFAST, SMASH

Virgos have a natural affinity for cooking and take great pleasure in preparing meals for others. Their meticulous nature shines in the kitchen, where they pay attention to detail and prioritise quality ingredients, ensuring that every dish is not only delicious but also beautifully presented. For Virgos, cooking is an act of love. It's not often that Virgos do things for themselves, as it's always about everyone else. So enjoy this drink and take time for you, for once.

MAKES 1 · GLASSWARE: TUMBLER
YOU WILL ALSO NEED A SPOON

- 25ML MALT WHISKY
- 15ML (1 TABLESPOON) MARTINI RISERVA SPECIALE RUBINO
- 15ML (1 TABLESPOON) BANANA LIQUEUR
- 5ML (1 TEASPOON) CINNAMON SYRUP
- 5ML (1 TEASPOON) MAPLE SYRUP
- 1 DASH OF BITTER TRUTH JERRY THOMAS BITTERS OR OTHER AROMATIC BITTERS
- ICE CUBES
- EGG GLASS (PAGE 22), TO GARNISH

Add all the ingredients to a Boston shaker including some ice cubes and stir for 30 seconds, or until condensation forms on the outside of the shaker.

Strain the cocktail through a fine strainer into a tumbler. Serve garnished with your Egg Glass and a spoon. Break the egg.

THE ANTIDOTE

TIKI, CITRUS, FIRE

So often Virgos can see much clearer than any other signs of the zodiac, so they can offer the perfect antidote for all negative situations and suggest a solution for all the emotional problems within others.

MAKES 1 · GLASSWARE: TANKARD OR HIGHBALL

- ICE CUBES
- 50ML PINEAPPLE JUICE
- 50ML CRANBERRY JUICE
- 25ML CITRIC ACID DILUTION (PAGE 14)
- 50ML FIRE SYRUP (PAGE 28)
- 50ML SODA WATER
- 2 PELLETS OF DRY ICE, TO GARNISH

Add ice cubes to your glass, pour in all the ingredients and lightly stir together.

Place the dry ice pellets on top. Wait for the dry ice to subside before consuming.

LIBRA

SCALES

AIR SIGN

7TH SIGN OF THE ZODIAC

CARDINAL ENERGY

RULING PLANET IS VENUS

Libra is the harmonious diplomat of the zodiac, embodying a deep appreciation for beauty and balance. Ruled by Venus, the planet of love and aesthetics, those born under this sign have an innate desire for harmony in relationships and their environment. They thrive on connection and often seek to create a peaceful atmosphere wherever they go. They strive for fairness and justice in all areas of the world, and they don't stop until they have achieved it.

As Libra season arrives, it ushers in a time of reflection and social engagement, celebrating the art of collaboration and cooperation. Libras approach life with charm and grace, effortlessly navigating social situations and fostering connections. When it comes to love, they are romantic and idealistic, valuing partnership and mutual respect above all.

While they may sometimes struggle with indecision and a tendency to avoid conflict, their diplomatic nature and appreciation for beauty truly shine. Mental rapport with others is especially important to them. They have a need to have someone tag along with them wherever they go — even if it is to the corner shop.

They simply can't help but see flaws in their environment and their relationships. In fact, anything out of whack will bother them until it's fixed.

COCKTAILS

TICKLE ME PINK

T&T

BRÛLÉE VOUS

POP NOTCH

AFFOGATO

NON-ALCOHOLIC

MARMALADE SPRITZ

TICKLE ME PINK

GIN, ELDERFLOWER, STING

Renowned for their stylish flair and feminine charm, Libras effortlessly embody elegance with the most remarkable way to curate outfits that reflect their personality, a keen eye for colour, textiles, textures and, of course, the best accessories.

MAKES 1 · GLASSWARE: ROCKS
YOU WILL ALSO NEED A SYRINGE

- 25ML GIN
- 15ML (1 TABLESPOON) ST-GERMAIN ELDERFLOWER LIQUEUR
- 15ML (1 TABLESPOON) LIME JUICE
- 15ML (1 TABLESPOON) SIMPLE SUGAR SYRUP (PAGE 21)

- 2 SHISO LEAVES
- ICE CUBES
- CRUSHED ICE
- 1ML ELECTRIC SYRUP (PAGE 22), TO GARNISH

Add the gin, elderflower liqueur, lime juice and sugar syrup to a Boston shaker with 1 ripped shiso leaf and some ice cubes and shake for 30 seconds, or until condensation forms on the outside of the shaker.

Add some crushed ice to a rocks glass, then strain the cocktail through a fine strainer into it.

Serve garnished with the remaining shiso leaf and the Electric Syrup.

T&T

TEQUILA, TONIC, FIRE

Libras sprinkle their own special magic into everything they do, effortlessly transforming the ordinary into the extraordinary! They have a natural talent for creating enchanting environments and making every interaction feel special.

**MAKES 1 · GLASSWARE: TEST TUBE OR FLUTE
YOU WILL ALSO NEED A TEST TUBE STAND**

- 25ML TEQUILA
- 15ML (1 TABLESPOON) PINK GRAPEFRUIT LIQUEUR
- 15ML (1 TABLESPOON) LIME JUICE
- 25ML FIRE SYRUP (PAGE 28)

- 50ML TONIC WATER
- ICE CUBES
- FLASH STRING (PAGE 10), TO GARNISH
- MINI WOODEN PEG, TO GARNISH
- 1 PELLET OF DRY ICE, TO GARNISH

Add the tequila, grapefruit liqueur, lime juice, Fire Syrup and tonic water to a Boston shaker with some ice cubes and stir for 30 seconds, or until condensation forms on the outside of the shaker.

Strain the cocktail through a fine strainer into a test tube, then using the peg, attach 10cm of flash string to the side of the test tube. Using a lighter, carefully light the bottom of the flash string. Once the string is no longer alight, remove the peg and add 1 pellet of dry ice to the top of the drink. Wait for the dry ice to subside before consuming.

We use flash paper and string, a favourite of magicians, to create added theatre in this drink.

BRÛLÉE VOUS

COGNAC, WHISKEY, CRÈME BRÛLÉE

With a natural inclination to people-please and ensure that everyone within their circle is happy, Libras often prioritise the wants and needs of others.

MAKES 1 · GLASSWARE: TUMBLER
YOU WILL ALSO NEED A BLOWTORCH AND AN ESPRESSO SPOON

- 15ML (1 TABLESPOON) MARTELL VS COGNAC
- 15ML (1 TABLESPOON) BUFFALO TRACE WHISKEY
- 15ML (1 TABLESPOON) LICOR 43
- 15ML (1 TABLESPOON) CRÈME BRÛLÈE SYRUP
- 50ML WHIPPING CREAM
- ICE CUBES
- MERINGUE FOAM (PAGE 33), TO GARNISH
- CASTER SUGAR, TO GARNISH

Add all the ingredients to a Boston shaker along with some ice cubes and shake for 30 seconds, or until condensation forms on the outside of the shaker.

Strain the cocktail through a fine strainer into a tumbler. Garnish with Meringue Foam level to the rim of your glass. Coat the foam with a good amount of caster sugar and use a blowtorch to caramelise the top.

Serve with an espresso spoon to crack the toasted foam and enjoy.

POP NOTCH

CHERRY, GINGER, POP

Libras are top-notch at everything they undertake, thanks to their natural charm, eye for detail and a strong sense of fairness. They have a diplomatic approach to everything and always support bringing situations back into harmony.

MAKES 1 · GLASSWARE: COUPE
YOU WILL ALSO NEED A FLAVOUR BLASTER

- 25ML WHITLEY NEILL BLACK CHERRY GIN
- 15ML (1 TABLESPOON) THE KING'S GINGER
- 25ML GRAPEFRUIT JUICE
- 50ML APPLE JUICE
- 15ML (1 TABLESPOON) LYCHEE SYRUP
- ICE CUBES

Add the gin, King's Ginger, grapefruit and apple juices and lychee syrup to a Boston shaker along with some ice cubes and stir for 30 seconds, or until condensation forms on the outside of the shaker.

Strain the cocktail through a fine strainer into a coupe glass. Garnish by adding a smoke bubble using your Flavour Blaster.

AFFOGATO

RUM, CARAMEL, COFFEE

With a taste for luxury and fine foods, Libras revel in great dining experiences and celebrate the beauty of life, making this cocktail perfect for those who are Venusian-ruled.

MAKES 1 · GLASSWARE: TUBO

- 25ML AMARO AVERNA
- 25ML COLD BREW COFFEE (PAGE 28)
- 25ML DISCARDED BANANA PEEL RUM
- 10ML (2 TEASPOONS) SALTED CARAMEL SYRUP
- 5ML (1 TEASPOON) AMARETTO
- ICE CUBES
- 1 WHITE CHOCOLATE ICE LOLLY (PAGE 24), TO GARNISH

Add the amaro, Coffee, rum, salted caramel syrup and amaretto to a Boston shaker along with some ice cubes and stir for 30 seconds, or until condensation forms on the outside of the shaker.

Strain the cocktail through a fine strainer into your glass.

To garnish, rest your White Chocolate Ice Lolly atop the glass.

MARMALADE SPRITZ

ORANGE, SODA, APERITIVE

Libras have a love for nice things. They are drawn to cool, fun environments, whether it's elegant home decor, fashionable clothing or exquisite art. They long for the finer things in life, making them connoisseurs of style. Libras often seek out items that not only enhance their surroundings but also reflect their sophisticated taste, believing that beauty can elevate everyday experiences and bring joy to their lives and the lives of those around them.

MAKES 1 · GLASSWARE: HIGHBALL

- 45ML (3 TABLESPOONS) EVERLEAF FOREST
- 3 TABLESPOONS ALCHEMIST MARMALADE (PAGE 14)
- 25ML CITRIC ACID DILUTION (PAGE 16)
- ICE CUBES
- 50ML SODA WATER

Add all the ingredients except the soda water to a Boston shaker along with some ice cubes and shake for 30 seconds, or until condensation forms on the outside of the shaker.

Pour directly into your glass and top up with soda water.

SCORPIO

SCORPION

WATER SIGN

8TH SIGN OF THE ZODIAC

FIXED ENERGY

RULING PLANET IS PLUTO

Scorpio is the intense transformer of the zodiac, embodying a powerful presence that captivates and intrigues! Ruled by Pluto, the planet of birth, death and transformation, those born under this sign possess a magnetic intensity and deep emotional depth as they navigate the ups and downs of their lives. They thrive on authenticity, and their magnetic personalities draw friends and relationships quickly and intensely.

Scorpio individuals approach life with a fierce determination, unafraid to explore the depths of their emotions and relationships. When it comes to love, they are passionate and loyal, forging deep connections that withstand the test of time. They are loyal until you betray them – that's when they have the ability to hold a grudge and walk away, without looking back.

With their understanding of the darkness of the human spirit and the depths of behaviours, they often seek to uncover hidden truths and mysteries, making them the psychologists of the zodiac. While they may sometimes struggle with jealousy and possessiveness, their strength and resilience truly shine. They are the strongest, most resilient sign of the zodiac, with a deep connection to the occult and all the ancient mysteries.

COCKTAILS

BITTER CHERRY
POISON APPLE
SMOKEY PALOMA
HARD PEACH ICED TEA
NEXT-SPRESSO MARTINI

NON-ALCOHOLIC

NOLOMA

BITTER CHERRY

TEQUILA, BITTER, CHERRY

Scorpios are known for their intense emotions and can hold a grudge with fierce determination, using their intuition to remember past betrayals long after others have moved on. This bitter drink is perfect for those moments.

MAKES 1 · GLASSWARE: BEAKER, CHILLED

- 25ML TEQUILA
- 25ML KAKUZO CHERRY BITTER
- 25ML STRAWBERRY SYRUP
- 25ML WATER

- ICE CUBES
- 1 MARASCHINO CHERRY, TO GARNISH
- SKULL PIN, TO GARNISH

Pour the tequila, Cherry Bitter, strawberry syrup and water into a Boston shaker along with some ice cubes and stir for 30 seconds, or until condensation forms on the outside of the shaker.

Strain the cocktail through a fine strainer into a chilled glass. Serve garnished with a maraschino cherry speared on a skull pin.

POISON APPLE

CALVADOS, TOFFEE, APPLE

Dating a Scorpio can be a tumultuous experience, as passion and emotional depth can sometimes border on possessiveness and jealousy. Their magnetic allure draws partners in, but this is an intense experience, as a Scorpio's love can feel intoxicating.

MAKES 1 · GLASSWARE: TUBO

- 25ML CALVADOS
- 25ML GREEN APPLE LIQUEUR
- 10ML (2 TEASPOONS) LIME SHERBET SYRUP
- 10ML (2 TEASPOONS) SALTED CARAMEL SYRUP
- 50ML WHITE WINE
- ICE CUBES
- 1 TOFFEE APPLE (PAGE 22), TO GARNISH

Add all the ingredients to a Boston shaker including some ice cubes and stir for 30 seconds, or until condensation forms on the outside of the shaker.

Strain the cocktail through a fine strainer into your glass then place the Toffee Apple into the glass.

SMOKEY PALOMA

TEQUILA, MANGO, SPICY

With an innate fascination with solving mysteries, Scorpios revel in uncovering hidden truths and navigating the intrigue of smoke and mirrors. Their sharp minds can decipher complex situations and see the layers in every situation.

MAKES 1 · GLASSWARE: HIGHBALL
YOU WILL ALSO NEED A BLOWTORCH

- ICE CUBES
- 25ML MANGO & CHILLI TEQUILA
- 25ML PAMPELLE RUBY APERÓ
- 5ML (1 TEASPOON) SIMPLE SUGAR SYRUP (PAGE 28)
- 150ML SCHÖFFERHOFER BEER
- 3 DEHYDRATED CITRUS WEDGES (PAGE 23), TO GARNISH
- SKULL PIN, TO GARNISH

Add some ice cubes to a highball glass, then add all the liquids and stir to mix well.

Garnish with the Dehydrated Citrus Wedges speared on a skull pin resting on the glass. Lightly blowtorch the citrus to colour and caramelise them, and serve.

HARD PEACH ICED TEA

WHISKEY, PEACH, TEA

The perfect drink for the strongest, most resilient sign of the zodiac. The ruling planet of Scorpios, Pluto, plunges them through birth, death and transformation many times throughout their life. Make a toast and celebrate how strong you are.

MAKES 1 · GLASSWARE: CONICAL AND ROCKS
YOU WILL ALSO NEED A BUNSEN BURNER AND TRIPOD

- 25ML MALT WHISKY
- 25ML PEACH LIQUEUR
- 15ML (1 TABLESPOON) CITRIC ACID DILUTION (PAGE 14)
- 10ML (2 TEASPOONS) AGAVE SYRUP
- 75ML SODA WATER

- 1 TEASPOON EARL GREY LOOSE LEAF TEA
- 1 TEASPOON MINT LOOSE LEAF TEA
- 0.1G METALLIC GOLD POWDER
- 2 PELLETS OF DRY ICE, TO GARNISH
- ICE CUBES

Add all the ingredients, except the dry ice and ice, to a pan over a medium heat on a bunsen burner and heat for 2 minutes to infuse. The liquid should be a nice warm temperature to serve.

Add the dry ice pellets to the conical flask.

Add some ice cubes to the rocks glass, pour in the cocktail through a tea strainer, then top with the dry ice. Wait for the dry ice to subside before consuming.

NEXT-SPRESSO MARTINI

COFFEE, CARAMEL, CAVIAR

With a fierce strength that allows them to walk away from those who hurt them or let them down, Scorpios value their own emotional wellbeing above all and won't tolerate betrayal in any way.

MAKES 1 · GLASSWARE: COUPE

- 25ML VODKA
- 15ML (1 TABLESPOON) SALTED CARAMEL SYRUP
- 15ML (1 TABLESPOON) COFFEE LIQUEUR
- 1 SHOT OF ESPRESSO
- ICE CUBES
- CHOCOLATE SPOON, TO GARNISH
- SALTED CARAMEL CAVIAR, TO GARNISH

Add the vodka, salted caramel syrup, coffee liqueur and espresso to a Boston shaker along with some ice cubes and hard shake for 30 seconds, or until condensation forms on the outside of the shaker.

Strain the cocktail through a fine strainer into your coupe glass, leaving a nice head on top of the drink. Garnish with a small Chocolate Spoon holding some Salted Caramel Caviar.

NOLOMA
GRAPEFRUIT, CITRUS, LIVENER

This cocktail sets the perfect stage for deep conversations and playful banter that Scorpios love. With its bold character, it invites you to dive into intriguing topics and share secrets that spark connection. Gather your soul mates and let the fun flow as you explore the depths of your thoughts.

MAKES 1 · GLASSWARE: HIGHBALL

- 25ML THREE SPIRIT LIVENER
- 10ML (2 TEASPOONS) GRAPEFRUIT SHERBET SYRUP
- 15ML (1 TABLESPOON) LIME JUICE
- 5ML (1 TEASPOON) AGAVE SYRUP
- 10ML (2 TEASPOONS) ALCHEMIST MARMALADE (PAGE 16)
- ICE CUBES
- 100ML SODA WATER
- 3 DEHYDRATED CITRUS WEDGES (PAGE 23), TO GARNISH

Add all the ingredients except the soda water to a Boston shaker including some ice cubes and shake for 30 seconds, or until condensation forms on the outside of the shaker.

Add ice cubes to your glass and strain in the cocktail through a fine strainer. Top with soda water.

Serve garnished with the Dehydrated Citrus Wedges.

SAGITTARIUS

ARCHER

FIRE SIGN

9TH SIGN OF THE ZODIAC

MUTABLE ENERGY

RULING PLANET IS JUPITER

Sagittarius are known for their adventurous spirit and boundless enthusiasm, always eager to explore new horizons and embrace life's experiences. They possess a strong sense of independence and freedom, often valuing their personal space and the ability to roam.

Their candidness and honesty can sometimes come off as blunt, but their infectious sense of humour and genuine warmth make them beloved companions. With a love for spontaneity, they often inspire others to step out of their comfort zones and join them on exciting escapades.

Ruled by Jupiter, the planet of expansion and abundance, those born under this sign possess an insatiable curiosity and a desire for new experiences. As Sagittarius season arrives, it ignites a sense of wanderlust and optimism, celebrating the joy of discovery and exploration.

Sagittarius individuals approach life with enthusiasm and a sense of humour, eager to embrace the unknown and share their insights with others. When it comes to love, they are open-minded and spirited, valuing freedom and growth in their relationships.

COCKTAILS

SEX ON THE PEACH

BEACH PLEASE

HIP FLASK JUNE BUG

PINEAPPLE PAVLOVA

PIÑA CO LAVA LAMP

NON-ALCOHOLIC

BANANA MANANA

SEX ON THE PEACH

VODKA, TROPICAL, PEACH

Sagittarius embody a free-spirited nature, revelling in the thrill of adventure and the exhilaration of spontaneity, which often leads them to seek out unconventional experiences. Their love for freedom drives them to embrace life's wild moments, making them the sign most likely to indulge in passionate encounters in the open air, where the beauty of nature enhances their sense of liberation and excitement. For them, every adventure is an opportunity to explore not just the world around them, but also the depths of their desires and connections.

MAKES 1 · GLASSWARE: COLLINS

- 15ML (1 TABLESPOON) VODKA
- 15ML (1 TABLESPOON) PEACH LIQUEUR
- 15ML (1 TABLESPOON) PASSOÃ
- 15ML (1 TABLESPOON) LEMON MIX (PAGE 14)
- 50ML PINEAPPLE JUICE
- 50ML CRANBERRY JUICE
- 1 DROP OF ULTRAFOAM
- ICE CUBES
- 25ML LONDON ESSENCE WHITE PEACH & JASMINE SODA
- SEASHELL, TO GARNISH
- MOLECULAR PEARL, TO GARNISH

Pour all the ingredients except the soda into a Boston shaker along with some ice cubes and shake for 30 seconds, or until condensation forms on the outside of the shaker.

Add some ice cubes to a collins glass and pour in the cocktail, through a fine strainer. Top with the peach soda and garnish with the pearl sat atop the seashell.

BEACH PLEASE

TEQUILA, CITRUS, BLUE

For Sagittarius, a day on the beach is the perfect blend of relaxation and adventure. Basking in the sun, swimming in the ocean and taking part in fun sports and activities on the beach help release some of their fiery competitive energy.

MAKES 1 · GLASSWARE: ROCKS

- 25ML TEQUILA
- 25ML LIME JUICE
- 15ML (1 TABLESPOON) BLUE CURAÇAO
- 15ML (1 TABLESPOON) APRICOT
  LIQUEUR
- 10ML (2 TEASPOONS) AGAVE SYRUP

- ICE CUBES
- SEA SALT, TO GARNISH
- YELLOW COLOURING POWDER,
  TO GARNISH
- LIME WEDGE, TO GARNISH
- ICE BALL

Add the tequila, lime juice, blue Curaçao, apricot liqueur and agave syrup to a Boston shaker along with some ice cubes and shake for 30 seconds, or until condensation forms on the outside of the shaker.

Mix equal amounts of salt and yellow powder on a plate. Coat the rim of a rocks glass with a lime wedge and roll through the powder to create a half rim. Add your ice ball to the rocks glass.

Strain the cocktail through a fine strainer into the rocks glass.

HIP FLASK JUNE BUG

GIN, BANANA, PINEAPPLE

Sagittarius thrive on adventure, constantly seeking the thrill of new experiences and the excitement of exploring uncharted territories, whether through travel, outdoor activities or daring pursuits that broaden their horizons. Surely you need a hip flask for all the adventures life offers you.

MAKES 1 · GLASSWARE: ROCKS
YOU WILL ALSO NEED A HIP FLASK

- 10ML BOMBAY SAPPHIRE PREMIER CRU
- 20ML BANANA LIQUEUR
- 20ML MIDORI
- 20ML PINEAPPLE AND COCONUT SYRUP
- 20ML CITRIC ACID DILUTION (PAGE 14)
- 12.5ML WATER
- ICE CUBES
- BANANA LEAF, TO GARNISH

Measure all the ingredients, except the ice cubes, into a jug and stir. Pour into a hip flask and place in the fridge to chill before serving.

When ready to serve, add some ice cubes to a rocks glass, pour in the cocktail through a fine strainer and serve garnished with a banana leaf.

PINEAPPLE PAVLOVA

PINEAPPLE, PEPPER, TOASTY

Sagittarius has an insatiable curiosity and a zest for life, eagerly embracing new experiences, exploring distant cultures or embarking on daring adventures that push the boundaries of the ordinary. With the 9th house ruling long-distance travel, they are most likely found exploring far-flung corners of the world.

MAKES 1 · GLASSWARE: COUPE
YOU WILL ALSO NEED A BLOWTORCH AND A SPOON

- 45ML (3 TABLESPOONS) PATRÓN REPOSADO TEQUILA
- 50ML PINEAPPLE JUICE
- 25ML LIME JUICE
- 25ML PEPPERCORN SYRUP (PAGE 31)
- ICE CUBES
- MERINGUE FOAM (PAGE 33), TO GARNISH

Add the tequila, pineapple and lime juices and Peppercorn Syrup to a Boston shaker along with some ice cubes and shake for 30 seconds, or until condensation forms on the outside of the shaker.

Strain the cocktail through a fine strainer into your glass and garnish with Meringue Foam. Lightly toast the foam with a blowtorch and serve with a spoon resting on top of the drink.

BANANA MANANA

BANANA, CHOCOLATE, MALT

A tropical delight crafted for the adventurous Sagittarius! With creamy vibes and a splash of holiday spirit, each sip feels like a sun-soaked getaway in a glass. Perfect for those wanderlust-filled days!

MAKES 1 · GLASSWARE: HIGHBALL

- 50ML APPLE JUICE
- 15ML (1 TABLESPOON) BANANA SYRUP
- 25ML MALT SYRUP (PAGE 18)
- 100ML WHITE CHOCOLATE FOAM (PAGE 32)
- ICE CUBES
- 25ML SODA WATER
- 3 BANANA SLICES, TO GARNISH

Add the apple juice, the banana and malt syrups and the White Chocolate Foam to a Boston shaker along with some ice cubes and shake for 30 seconds, or until condensation forms on the outside of the shaker.

Add ice cubes to your glass and strain in the cocktail through a fine strainer. Top up with soda water. Serve garnished with the banana slices.

PIÑA CO LAVA LAMP

RUM, COCONUT, CAVIAR

With a perpetual need to seek knowledge and adventure, it's no surprise that Sagittarius would be the zodiac sign most eager to rub the lamp to unlock new realms of wisdom and experience the magic of the unknown.

MAKES 1 · GLASSWARE: TEST TUBE OR HIGHBALL
YOU WILL ALSO NEED AN LED LIGHT AND A TEST TUBE STAND

- 15ML (1 TABLESPOON) CITRIC ACID DILUTION (PAGE 14)
- 15ML (1 TABLESPOON) PINEAPPLE LIQUEUR
- 15ML (1 TABLESPOON) COCONUT RUM
- 5ML (1 TEASPOON) JAMAICAN RUM
- 50ML PROSECCO
- 5ML (1 TEASPOON) SIMPLE SUGAR SYRUP (PAGE 21)
- ICE CUBES
- 1 PELLET OF DRY ICE, TO GARNISH
- 1 TEASPOON PINEAPPLE CAVIAR (PAGE 17), TO GARNISH

Add the Citric Acid Dilution, pineapple liqueur, both the rums, the prosecco and the Sugar Syrup to a Boston shaker along with some ice cubes and stir for 30 seconds, or until condensation forms on the outside of the shaker.

Add your LED light to the base of your test tube stand. Strain the cocktail through a fine strainer into the test tube and add the dry ice pellet. Garnish with a teaspoon of Pineapple Caviar and wait for the dry ice to subside before consuming.

CAPRICORN

SEA GOAT

EARTH SIGN

10TH SIGN OF THE ZODIAC

MUTABLE ENERGY

RULING PLANET IS SATURN

Capricorn is the disciplined architect of the zodiac, embodying a strong sense of responsibility and ambition. Ruled by Saturn, the planet of structure and discipline, those born under this sign possess a practical mindset and a determination to achieve their goals. They thrive on hard work and often seek to build a secure and successful future.

While Capricorns are often seen as serious and focused individuals, they also have a playful and humorous side. They enjoy a good laugh and lighten the mood with their witty remarks. However, they may sometimes struggle with expressing their emotions and may come across as reserved or distant.

As Capricorn season unfolds, it brings a sense of purpose and focus, celebrating the value of perseverance and dedication. Capricorn individuals approach life with a serious demeanour, driven to excel in their endeavours and create lasting legacies. When it comes to love, they are loyal and devoted, valuing stability and commitment in their relationships.

Capricorn personalities are ambitious and pragmatic, ready to lead and inspire others with their unwavering determination and strong leadership.

COCKTAILS

PIPE DREAM

BALL BREAKER

ELDERPOWER

FESTIVE BELLINI

PRESSURISED CHOC-O-GRONI

NON-ALCOHOLIC

POWER TRIP

PIPE DREAM

SMOKEY, CHOCOLATE, OPULENCE

Ruling the 10th house of career and public life, Capricorns are driven by a relentless ambition to climb the ladder of success, always striving for bigger and better opportunities in their lives. Their strong work ethic, discipline and determination propel them to set lofty goals and pursue them with unwavering focus, ensuring they leave a lasting impact in their professional endeavours and personal achievements.

MAKES 1 · GLASSWARE: PIPESHAPED OR NICK & NORA, CHILLED

- 25ML DARK RUM
- 15ML (1 TABLESPOON) LICOR 43
- 15ML (1 TABLESPOON) DISCARDED SWEET CASCARA VERMOUTH
- 5ML (1 TEASPOON) LAPHROAIG 10-YEAR, OR ANY SMOKEY AND PEATY WHISKY
- 25ML CHOCOLATE COOKIE SYRUP
- ICE CUBES

Pour all the ingredients into a Boston shaker including some ice cubes and stir for 30 seconds, or until condensation forms on the outside of the shaker.

Strain the cocktail through a fine strainer into the chilled glass.

BALL BREAKER

GIN, BLACKCURRANT, SPHERE

Capricorns are relentless achievers in both work and life, known for their no-nonsense approach and high standards that challenge everyone around them to step up and reach their fullest potential. They are ruled by Saturn, the planet renowned as the disciplinarian of the zodiac, which symbolises responsibility, structure and long-term goals.

MAKES 1 · GLASSWARE: ROCKS

- CRUSHED ICE
- 25ML GIN
- 25ML PINK GRAPEFRUIT LIQUEUR
- 25ML LEMON MIX (PAGE 14)
- 5ML (1 TEASPOON) SIMPLE SUGAR SYRUP (PAGE 21)
- BLACKCURRANT BALL (PAGE 23), TO GARNISH

Add some crushed ice to a rocks glass, then pour in the gin, grapefruit liqueur, Lemon Mix and Sugar Syrup. Using a spoon, gently stir to mix.

Add a small cap of crushed ice on the top of the drink and garnish with your Blackcurrant Ball. Serve and pop the ball.

ELDERPOWER

ELDERFLOWER, VODKA, VIBRANCE

Capricorns exude a remarkable sense of power and authority, rooted in their determination, discipline and strategic mindset. Their strong ambition drives them to set high goals and pursue them with a relentless focus, often positioning Capricorns as natural leaders in both their personal and professional spheres. With an innate ability to navigate challenges and setbacks, Capricorns demonstrate resilience and practicality, inspiring others with their steadfastness and commitment to success.

MAKES 1 · GLASSWARE: CAN OR HIGHBALL

- 25ML ST-GERMAIN ELDERFLOWER LIQUEUR
- 15ML (1 TABLESPOON) DUTCH BARN VODKA
- 10ML (2 TEASPOONS) ALCHEMIST MARMALADE (PAGE 16)
- 15ML (1 TABLESPOON) CUCUMBER AND MINT SYRUP (PAGE 30)
- ICE CUBES
- 50ML PROSECCO
- 50ML SODA WATER
- CRUSHED ICE
- DRAGON FRUIT POWDER, TO GARNISH

Add the elderflower liqueur, vodka, Marmalade and Syrup to a Boston shaker along with some ice cubes and shake for 30 seconds, or until condensation forms on the outside of the shaker.

Pour the prosecco and soda water into the shaker.

Add some ice cubes to your glass. Strain the cocktail into the glass and top with a cap of crushed ice. Serve garnished with a dusting of dragon fruit powder.

FESTIVE BELLINI

WINE, SPICE, GLITTER

If you're a Capricorn, your birthday falls right around the festive season, often near Christmas, which adds an extra layer of magic to your celebrations. Celebrate yourself and all the success you have achieved and set the stage for new goals and aspirations in the year ahead. This time of year is filled with joy, warmth and a spirit of giving, reflecting the generous nature of Capricorns.

MAKES 1 · GLASSWARE: FLUTE

— 25ML MULLED BELLINI BATCH (PAGE 16)
— 50ML PROSECCO

Pour both the ingredients into a flute and serve.

PRESSURISED CHOC-O-GRONI
GIN, CHOCOLATE, BITTERS

Capricorns thrive under pressure, showcasing their remarkable ability to remain calm and focused when faced with challenges. Their practical nature and strong problem-solving skills enable them to assess situations critically and devise effective strategies, making them invaluable in high-stakes environments.

MAKES 1 · GLASSWARE: WE USE A DRESCHEL BOTTLE AND A 250ML BEAKER TO CREATE THE PRESSURE. A ROCKS GLASS WOULD WORK AS AN ALTERNATIVE

- 25ML GIN
- 25ML MARTINI RISERVA SPECIALE RUBINO VERMOUTH OR OTHER SWEET VERMOUTH
- 15ML (1 TABLESPOON) CAMPARI
- 15ML (1 TABLESPOON) GRAND MARNIER
- 10ML (2 TEASPOONS) CHOCOLATE COOKIE SYRUP
- 1 DASH OF BITTER TRUTH JERRY THOMAS CHOCOLATE BITTERS OR OTHER AROMATIC BITTERS
- ICE CUBES
- 1 PELLET OF DRY ICE, TO GARNISH

Add all the ingredients except the dry ice to a Boston shaker including some ice cubes and stir for 30 seconds, or until condensation forms on the outside of the shaker.

Strain the drink through a fine strainer into the lower compartment of the Dreschel bottle. Add 1 pellet of dry ice to the top chamber of the Dreschel bottle.

Fill your beaker with ice cubes. Applying pressure to one side of the Dreschel bottle with your finger should force the liquid out into your beaker. Wait for the dry ice to subside before consuming.

POWER TRIP

ORANGE, ROSEMARY, CBD

Capricorns have a natural affinity for power and authority, often driven by their ambition to achieve success and make a meaningful impact in their personal and professional lives. They are motivated by the desire to take charge and influence their surroundings, using their strong work ethic and strategic thinking to climb the ranks and secure leadership roles.

MAKES 1 · GLASSWARE: ROCKS

- 15ML (1 TABLESPOON) LIME SHERBET SYRUP
- 15ML (1 TABLESPOON) ELDERFLOWER SYRUP
- 125ML TRIP BLOOD ORANGE AND ROSEMARY

- ICE CUBES
- GINGER FOAM (PAGE 32), TO GARNISH
- CBD GUMMIE, TO GARNISH
- SKULL PIN, TO GARNISH

Add both the syrups and the Trip blend to a Boston shaker along with some ice cubes and stir for 30 seconds, or until condensation forms on the outside of the shaker.

Add some ice cubes to your glass and strain in the cocktail through a fine strainer. Garnish with Ginger Foam and top with a CBD gummie speared on a skull pin.

AQUARIUS

WATER BEARER

AIR SIGN

11TH SIGN OF THE ZODIAC

FIXED ENERGY

RULING PLANET IS URANUS

Here come the freedom fighters, the community makers and the free spirits. In 2020 we shifted into the Age of Aquarius, so Aquarians have a job to do on this planet, and they will make it happen.

Aquarians can struggle to make changes in their own life and can often be misunderstood, seen as aloof and withdrawn. However, while it can take time for them to find 'their people', for Aquarians, once a bond forms they become the most loyal friend, who will fight for the underdog, for change and independence. There is an innate understanding of the need for change within the world, and technology is how Aquarians envision that change, embracing new technology and gadgets.

As Aquarius season arrives, it ushers in a wave of creativity and unconventional thinking, celebrating the beauty of individuality and freedom. These individuals approach life with an open mind, eager to explore new concepts and connect with like-minded souls. When it comes to love, they are independent and unconventional, valuing friendship and intellectual stimulation in their relationships.

While they may sometimes struggle with emotional detachment and unpredictability, their originality and humanitarian spirit will truly shine.

COCKTAILS

FLASH GORDON

BUBBLE TEA

JÄGER BOMB

HAZELNUT NEBULA

PLANT POT PICANTE

NON-ALCOHOLIC

EUREKA MOMENT

FLASH GORDON

GINGER, PLUM, SCOTCH

This iconic space hero embodies all the traits of a true Aquarius, driven by a unique perspective and a desire for freedom. Flash's adventures across the cosmos reflect the Aquarian spirit of innovation and rebellion against tyranny.

MAKES 1 · GLASSWARE: TUBO

- 50ML GLENMORANGIE X
- 5ML (1 TEASPOON) THE KING'S GINGER
- 25ML PLUM & HONEY SYRUP (PAGE 30)
- 25ML LEMON MIX (PAGE 14)
- ICE CUBES
- FLASH PAPER (PAGE 10), TO GARNISH
- SKULL PIN, TO GARNISH

Add all the liquid ingredients to a Boston shaker along with some ice cubes and shake for 30 seconds, or until condensation forms on the outside of the shaker.

Strain the cocktail through a fine strainer into your glass.

To garnish, add a small piece of flash paper (roughly the size of a small flag) to a skull pin and let it rest in the glass. When ready, safely use a lighter to light the bottom of the flash paper.

BUBBLE TEA

PEACH, JASMINE, BOBA

Aquarians are often viewed as beings from other planets. Bubble tea is the perfect drink for futuristic Aquarius, merging creativity and innovation in every sip. With its vibrant colours, unique flavours and playful tapioca pearls, bubble tea reflects the Aquarian spirit of individuality and experimentation.

MAKES 1 · GLASSWARE: HIGHBALL
YOU WILL ALSO NEED A BOBA STRAW

- 25ML TEQUILA
- 15ML (1 TABLESPOON) PEACH LIQUEUR
- 25ML CITRIC ACID DILUTION (PAGE 14)
- 25ML MANGO SYRUP
- ½ TEASPOON SALINE SOLUTION (PAGE 30)

- 50ML LONDON ESSENCE WHITE PEACH & JASMINE SODA
- ICE CUBES
- APPLE BOBA, TO GARNISH
- 1 PELLET OF DRY ICE, TO GARNISH (OPTIONAL)

Add the tequila, peach liqueur, Citric Acid Dilution, mango syrup, Saline Solution and peach and jasmine soda to a Boston shaker along with some ice cubes and stir for 30 seconds, or until condensation forms on the outside of the shaker.

Strain the cocktail through a fine strainer into your glass and serve with your apple boba and a boba straw. If you like, top with a pellet of dry ice — but you must wait for it to subside before drinking.

JÄGER BOMB

JÄGERMEISTER, PEACH, BOOM

Aquarians are often seen as catalysts for change in their communities. As rulers of the 11th house of community, they utilise their sharp intellect and innovative ideas to 'drop bombs' of inspiration and action that challenge the status quo. With a deep-seated belief in equality and social justice, they aren't afraid to confront difficult issues head on, sparking conversations that encourage others to think critically and embrace new perspectives.

MAKES 1 · GLASSWARE: 250ML ROUND BOTTOM FLASK OR A ROCKS GLASS AS AN ALTERNATIVE

- 45ML (3 TABLESPOONS) JÄGERMEISTER
- 30ML GIFFARD CRÈME DE PÊCHE OR OTHER PEACH CREAM
- 10 MINT LEAVES
- 22.5ML LEMON JUICE

- 40ML SODA WATER
- ICE CUBES
- MINI WOODEN PEG, TO GARNISH
- FLASH STRING (PAGE 10), TO GARNISH

Add all the ingredients to a Boston shaker along with ice cubes and shake for 30 seconds, or until condensation forms on the outside of the shaker.

Using a fine strainer, pour the drink into a glass.

Using the peg, attach 10cm of flash string to the rim of the glass and with a lighter carefully set the end of the string furthest away from the glass alight.

HAZELNUT NEBULA

ORANGE, HAZELNUT, CREAM

Embodying the qualities of mystery, creativity and potential. Just as nebulae are vast clouds of gas and dust that serve as nurseries for new stars, Aquarians are often seen as the source of innovative ideas and inspiration. They possess a unique ability to bring together diverse thoughts and perspectives, much like the varied elements found within a nebula.

MAKES 1 · GLASSWARE: NICK & NORA

- 25ML GRAND MARNIER
- 25ML FRANGELICO LIQUEUR
- 10ML (2 TEASPOONS) VANILLA SYRUP
- 25ML WHIPPING CREAM
- 25ML MILK
- ICE CUBES
- RICE PAPER TOPPER, TO GARNISH

Add all the ingredients to a Boston shaker along with some ice cubes and shake for 30 seconds, or until condensation forms on the outside of the shaker.

Strain the cocktail through a fine strainer into your glass and garnish with a rice paper topper.

PLANT POT PICANTE

TEQUILA, SMOKEY, SPICE

We know Aquarians have a remarkable ability to find their tribe, often seeking out like-minded individuals who share their values of innovation, freedom and social justice. You are drawn to people who appreciate unique perspectives and embrace their unconventional nature. When Aquarians connect with their 'people', it's as if they discover a cosmic alignment that feels effortless and natural, like peas in a pod.

MAKES 1 · GLASSWARE: TERRACOTTA POT OR HIGHBALL

- 25ML REPOSADO TEQUILA
- 25ML MEZCAL VERDE
- 25ML LIME JUICE
- 15ML (1 TABLESPOON) GRAPEFRUIT JUICE
- 10ML (2 TEASPOONS) AGAVE SYRUP
- 5ML (1 TEASPOON) GOCHUJANG PASTE

- ICE CUBES
- SALT AND PEPPER SEASONING (CAN BE FOUND IN ASIAN SUPERMARKETS), TO GARNISH
- MIXED PICKLES (WE USE BABY ONIONS, CHILLIS, OLIVES AND CORNICHONS), TO GARNISH
- SKULL PIN OR TOOTHPICK

Add the tequila, mezcal, lime and grapefruit juices, agave syrup and gochujang paste to a Boston shaker along with some ice cubes and stir for 30 seconds, or until condensation forms on the outside of the shaker.

Pour some salt and pepper seasoning on a plate and use a lime wedge to create a stripe down the side of the terracotta pot. Roll the rim through the seasoning. Then add some ice cubes and strain in the cocktail through a fine strainer. Add your olives, pickled onion, cornichon and chilli to your cocktail pin. Balance on top of your drink.

EUREKA MOMENT

LEMON, GINGER, SMOKE

The true creators of eureka moments, Aquarians are known for their forward-thinking mindset and innovative spirit, making them adept at finding the easiest ways to improve life through technology and exploration.

**MAKES 1 · GLASSWARE: ROCKS AND CONICAL FLASK
YOU WILL ALSO NEED A BUNSEN BURNER AND TRIPOD**

- 25ML THREE SPIRIT LIVENER
- 15ML (1 TABLESPOON) LEMON MIX (PAGE 14)
- 15ML (1 TABLESPOON) RASPBERRY SYRUP
- 100ML GINGER BEER
- 2 MINT SPRIGS
- 2 PELLETS OF DRY ICE, TO GARNISH
- ICE CUBES

Add the livener, Lemon Mix, raspberry syrup and ginger beer to a pan over a medium heat on a bunsen burner and heat gently for 2 minutes. Remove from the heat, add a mint sprig and leave to infuse and cool. The liquid should be a nice warm temperature to serve.

Add the dry ice pellets to your conical flask.

Fill a glass with ice cubes and add a mint sprig. Discard the mint sprig from the cocktail mix then pour the drink into the glass. Add the dry ice, then wait for it to subside before consuming.

PISCES

FISH

WATER SIGN

12TH SIGN OF THE ZODIAC

MUTABLE ENERGY

RULING PLANET IS NEPTUNE

Pisces are the floaty, dreamy empaths of the zodiac, often late when you make plans with them as they are walking round in a daze looking for things. They embody a mystical essence that flows with creativity and compassion!

Ruled by Neptune, the planet of dreams and intuition, those born under this sign possess a deep emotional sensitivity and a rich imagination. They thrive on a deep connection and often seek to heal and uplift those around them through their nurturing, caring energy.

It's said they are the wise ones, and this wisdom brings the ability to intuitively feel other people's emotions, pain and feelings. Being able to read what other people are feeling can be very heavy and draining for their sensitive systems. Pisces, like all the other water signs, need alone time for self-care, to process their own emotions and to discover if what they feel is theirs or they are carrying the pain of others around them.

Pisces individuals approach life with a gentle spirit, eager to explore the realms of fantasy and spirituality. When it comes to love, they are romantic and selfless, often putting the needs of others before their own. While they may sometimes struggle with boundaries and escapism, their empathy and creativity truly shine.

COCKTAILS

BARREL-AGED PINEAPPLE DAIQUIRI
HOLY SMOKES
LOST IN TRANSLATION
MARTINI IN A BOTTLE
BERLIN BUBBLES

NON-ALCOHOLIC

DARK FRUITS

BARREL-AGED PINEAPPLE DAIQUIRI

RUM, PINEAPPLE, AGED

Pisces are often considered the oldest souls in the zodiac, embodying a deep well of wisdom and understanding that comes from their intuitive nature and rich emotional experiences. With an innate ability to connect with the collective consciousness, they carry the lessons of the past and possess a profound empathy for others.

MAKES 1 · GLASSWARE: NICK & NORA
YOU WILL ALSO NEED A 1LITRE BARREL

- 350ML PINEAPPLE RUM
- 350ML PINEAPPLE LIQUEUR
- 165ML CITRIC ACID DILUTION (PAGE 14)
- 90ML PINEAPPLE AND COCONUT SYRUP
- ICE CUBES
- DEHYDRATED PINEAPPLE CRISP, TO GARNISH

Measure out the rum, pineapple liqueur, Citric Acid Dilution and pineapple and coconut syrup and add to the barrel. Once all the ingredients are added, rotate the barrel often and leave to age as long as you want.

To serve, measure out 100ml from the barrel and add to a Boston shaker along with some ice cubes and stir for 30 seconds.

Strain the cocktail through a fine strainer into a Nick & Nora glass and garnish with a dehydrated pineapple crisp.

HOLY SMOKES

BANANA, PINEAPPLE, SMOKE

The soulful depth found in every Pisces allows them to navigate life's complexities with grace, often seeing beyond the surface to grasp the underlying truths of human existence. Their compassionate spirit and introspective qualities make them wise beyond their years, guiding others with their insights and offering a unique sense of knowing. They are said to be the closest connected to a higher consciousness.

MAKES 1 · GLASSWARE: ROCKS
YOU WILL ALSO NEED A 250ML CONICAL FLASK, A SMOKE GUN AND SOME OAK WOODCHIPS

- 25ML MEZCAL
- 15ML (1 TABLESPOON) BANANA LIQUEUR
- 15ML (1 TABLESPOON) BANANA SYRUP
- 15ML (1 TABLESPOON) CITRIC ACID DILUTION (PAGE 14)
- 50ML PINEAPPLE JUICE
- ICE CUBES

Add the mezcal, banana liqueur, banana syrup, Citric Acid Dilution and pineapple juice to a Boston shaker along with some ice cubes and shake for 30 seconds, or until condensation forms on the outside of the shaker.

Strain the cocktail through a fine strainer into your conical flask.

Prepare a rocks glass with ice cubes. Add the woodchips to your smoke gun and smoke your conical flask, then pour into the glass. Wait for the smoke to subside before consuming.

LOST IN TRANSLATION

LIME, VODKA, DISCO FOAM

These dreamers and visionaries are often overwhelmed in this crazy world where it is so easy to be misunderstood, and they can struggle to articulate their complex emotions and express their thoughts and feelings clearly.

MAKES 1 · GLASSWARE: NICK & NORA

- 25ML MAKRUT LIME LEAF-INFUSED VODKA (PAGE 27)
- 25ML MOUSE KINGDOM DARK BERRIES LIQUEUR
- 25ML LEMON MIX (PAGE 14)
- 10ML (2 TEASPOONS) BRISTOL SYRUP COMPANY DISCO GRENADINE
- 25ML STRAWBERRY PURÉE
- ICE CUBES
- BASIL FOAM (PAGE 34), TO GARNISH
- GROUND BLACK PEPPER, TO GARNISH

Add the vodka, berry liqueur, Lemon Mix, grenadine and strawberry purée to a Boston shaker along with some ice cubes and shake for 30 seconds, or until condensation forms on the outside of the shaker.

Strain the cocktail through a fine strainer into your glass and garnish with the Basil Foam. Finish with a light dusting of black pepper.

MARTINI IN A BOTTLE
VODKA, PASSIONFRUIT, GLITTER

Pisces are likely to send a message in a bottle, embodying their whimsical and romantic nature. With a desire for connection and expression, they may craft heartfelt notes filled with their dreams, hopes or feelings, and release them into the ocean or a river, symbolising their longing to reach someone who understands their soul.

MAKES 1 · GLASSWARE: COUPE
YOU WILL ALSO NEED A SCREWTOP BOTTLE WITH A LID OR STRAW

- 15ML (1 TABLESPOON) VODKA
- 25ML PASSOÃ
- 25ML CITRIC ACID DILUTION (PAGE 14)
- 10ML (2 TEASPOONS) PASSIONFRUIT SYRUP
- 10ML (2 TEASPOONS) VANILLA SYRUP
- 75ML WATER
- 75ML WHITE WINE
- 0.5G RED COLOURING POWDER
- 0.5G METALLIC SILVER POWDER

Add all the ingredients to a measuring jug and stir thoroughly.

Pour into your bottle and screw the lid shut. Chill before serving and drink straight out of the bottle using a straw or decant into a coupe glass.

DARK FRUITS

PASSIONFRUIT, POMEGRANATE, FIZZ

When the garnish is a bath bomb ... Pisces loves baths as a serene escape, immersing themselves in warm water to wash away the stresses of the day and indulge in a dreamy, soothing sanctuary for their sensitive spirit.

MAKES 1 · GLASSWARE: HIGHBALL

- ICE CUBES
- 15ML (1 TABLESPOON) PASSIONFRUIT SYRUP
- 1 BOTTLE DOUBLE DUTCH POMEGRANATE & BASIL SODA
- 1 BATH BOMB (PAGE 23)

Fill your glass with ice cubes, then add the passionfruit syrup and soda and lightly stir.

Drop in your Bath Bomb to serve.

BERLIN BUBBLES

LEMONGRASS, CARDAMON, BUBBLES

A dreamy escape in a glass, this playful cocktail fizzes like a bubble bath. Inspired by the intuitive and imaginative nature of Pisces, it's a drink for daydreamers, delicate, otherworldly and impossible to forget.

MAKES 1 · GLASSWARE: COUPE

- 52.5ML TANQUERAY PARADISO
- 15ML (1 TABLESPOON) LIME JUICE
- 15ML (1 TABLESPOON) CARDAMOM SYRUP (PAGE 31)
- 1 DASH OF ORANGE BITTERS
- ICE CUBES
- 1 PELLET OF DRY ICE, TO GARNISH

Add the Tanqueray, lime juice, Cardamom Syrup and orange bitters to a Boston glass along with some ice cubes and shake with the Boston tin.

Add a drop of water to a coupe glass to wet the bottom, then add a pellet of dry ice, and use a muddler to crush the dry ice pellet to the bottom of the glass. Using a fine strainer, pour the drink into the coupe. Wait for the dry ice to subside before consuming.

GLOSSARY

BITTERS

An alcoholic liquid flavoured with herbs and plants. Bitters were originally developed for medicinal purposes, but they are now widely used as a cocktail ingredient.

CALCIUM LACTATE POWDER

Calcium lactate is a type of salt. It has various uses, including as a firming agent in some foods, but in molecular gastronomy it is used in the spherification and reverse spherification processes (page 23) because of the way it reacts with sodium alginate, causing a skin to form.

CITRIC ACID POWDER

Citric acid is found naturally in citrus fruits, especially lemons and limes. In its powdered form, it is used as flavour enhancer and can also be used as an emulsifying agent to prevent fats from separating. We use it in our Citric Acid Dilution (page 14) as a way of adding a citrus flavour boost to a drink without affecting the colour or making the liquid cloudy in the way that adding fresh citrus juice will.

COLOUR POWDERS

High-strength food colourings that pack a powerful punch and mix well into almost any batch or liquid. A little goes a very long way.

FLAVOUR DROPS

Similar to essences that you would use in cooking, these flavour drops are intensely flavoured and provide a lot of taste in very small amounts.

ISOMALT

A sugar substitute created from sucrose. It resists crystallisation.

MALT EXTRACT

A thick liquid syrup derived from barley grains and water. It has a sweet, distinctive flavour.

MSK ULTRAGEL

A vegan, seaweed-based gelling agent, this is perfect for use in jellies, such as our Strawberry Jelly on (page 17).

SODIUM ALGINATE

Alginate is a substance extracted from algae. It's known for its ability to hold water, making it a natural gelling agent. It's food-safe and is used as a thickening/gelling agent in jellies, ice creams, etc.

UTRAFOAM DROPS

UltraFoam is a high-performance, natural, plant-based foaming agent, which you can use to create a very stable and long-lasting light, airy foam on a liquid.

ULTRATEX POWDER

A gluten-free thickening starch.

XANTHAN GUM

Produced from simple sugars through a fermentation process, xanthan gum is used as a thickening agent in some of our foams and flavour mixes.

RESOURCES

BITTER TRUTH
the-bitter-truth.com

BRISTOL SYRUP COMPANY
bristolsyrupcompany.com

EASY MAGIC
easymagic.co.uk

EVOLVED FOODS
evolvedfoods.co.uk

FLAVOUR BLASTER
flavourblaster.com

IMAGINATIVE CUISINE
imaginativecuisine.com

KITCHEQUIP
kitchequip.co.uk

MONIN SYRUPS
monin1912.com

MSK INGREDIENTS
msk-ingredients.com

PEARLS MOLECULAR EXPERIENCE
molecularexperience.com

SHOUT DRY ICE
shoutdryice.co.uk

SPECIAL INGREDIENTS
specialingredients.co.uk

INDEX

ACKNOWLEDGMENTS

This book is dedicated to all of our Alchemists. The brilliant teams that work under the sun and under the moon to deliver the many thousands of cosmic cocktails each week, and to the supporting cast in operations, and in our base, whose energy and efforts are unsurpassed in their pursuit of excellence.

Among that galaxy of superstars we'd like to acknowledge a few who have burned brightest over the last few years.

To Jonny, who has squared the (magic) circle; marrying effervescent charisma with organisational rigour, strengthening industry ties and driving drinks quality since he was passed the torch in 2022.

To John, who has brought great humour and some canny objectivity to the operation.

To Hannah and Arron for their boundless energy and the passionate personality that embodies The Collective spirit(s).

To Mark, Michelle, Vic and Mitch for navigating a path through the highs and lows of the last few years and for their dedication to the business of Alchemy.

And to Hannah #1, from whom all that is great and good about the many, many people of The Alchemist flows.

You are reading this book because Jenny willed it; her character and creativity have taken The Alchemist brand out of this world and into a new realm, and the project to commit that journey to these pages would not have happened without her direction.

We praise Charlotte, the Moon Witch. Our friend and guide through the stars who helped manifest the zodiac journey and for all her support both in these pages and all along The Alchemist path.

Thanks again to Hannah and to Nicky for their patience and persistence during the shoot as the concoctions were committed to celluloid.

To Izzy and Elizabeth at Ebury and the wider Penguin team for their cheerleading and support throughout what has been an equally thrilling process in making the vision in these pages a reality.

Our cocktailing collective has contributed much in terms of recipes here, but a special mention must go to Aiden, who has taken the spirit and the spirits to a new world of theatre in Berlin, adding some Teutonic tipples to tickle your tastebuds.

And finally, we salute you, dear reader. We thank you for your patronage and your engagement — we love seeing and hearing about your experiences with our drinks as we've taken them further and wider — shaking tins in Singapore, Dubai and Berlin. We look forward to many more interactions in this cosmos or the next.

Love and Theatre

EBURY PRESS

UK | USA | Canada | Ireland | Australia
India | New Zealand | South Africa

Ebury Press is part of the Penguin Random House group
of companies whose addresses can be found at global.
penguinrandomhouse.com

Penguin Random House UK
One Embassy Gardens, 8 Viaduct Gardens,
London SW11 7BW

penguin.co.uk
global.penguinrandomhouse.com

The authorised representative in the EEA is
Penguin Random House Ireland, Morrison Chambers,
32 Nassau Street, Dublin D02 YH68.

A CIP catalogue record for this book is available
from the British Library

ISBN 9781529958348

Penguin Random House is committed to a sustainable
future for our business, our readers and our planet.
This book is made from Forest Stewardship Council®
certified paper.

MIX
Paper from
responsible sources
FSC® C018179

First published by Ebury Press in 2025
1

Publishing Director: Elizabeth Bond
Assistant Editor: Izzy Frost
Production Controller: Percie Bridgwater
Designer: Sandra Zellmer
Photographer: Haarala Hamilton
Prop Stylist: Jenny Iggledon

Colour origination by Altaimage Ltd
Printed and bound in Italy by LEGO SpA